Praise for *Presentation Zen: Simple Ideas on Presentation Design and Delivery, Second Edition*

"It's often the slim books that have the most impact. Strunk and White for proper English. *Robert's Rules of Order* for running meetings. Both deceptively short, with huge impact. To these I find it easy to add *Presentation Zen* for moving an audience. Embrace this wonderful guide and gain the power of crafting simple and clear messages. Garr Reynolds provides techniques and examples in a manner that, quite naturally, adheres to the same principles as what he teaches."

—**Ric Bretschneider**, Senior Program Manager,
PowerPoint Development Team 1993-2010

"Garr is a beacon of hope for frustrated audiences everywhere. His design philosophy and fundamental principles bring life to messages and can invigorate careers. His principles of simplicity are as much a journey of the soul as they are restraint of the mouse."

—**Nancy Duarte**, CEO, Duarte, Inc., and
author of *slide:ology* and *resonate*

"*Presentation Zen* changed my life and the lives of my clients. As a communications specialist, I was searching for a way to create visuals that support the narrative without detracting from the story. The philosophy and approach so elegantly explained in Garr's book will inspire your audience. Don't even think of giving another presentation without it!"

—**Carmine Gallo**, author of *The Presentation
Secrets of Steve Jobs*

"Garr has broken new ground in the way we think about the power of presentations, and more important, has taught an entire generation of communicators how to do a better job. Don't miss this one."

—**Seth Godin**, legendary presenter
and author of *We Are All Weird*

"If you care about the quality and clarity of your presentations—and you should—pick up this book, read every page, and heed its wisdom. *Presentation Zen* is a contemporary classic."

—**Daniel H. Pink**, author of
Drive and *A Whole New Mind*

"Four years ago, Garr's *Presentation Zen* literally changed the world of communications. Almost overnight, what was once fluffy, stale, and boring became sharp, brisk, and even (can we say it?) fun. A million radically-improved speeches later, the world is ready for a refresher—and just when we need it most, Garr delivers the magic again."

—**Dan Roam**, author of *Blah-Blah-Blah*
and *The Back of the Napkin*

presentation zen

Simple Ideas on Presentation Design and Delivery

New Riders

Garr Reynolds

Presentation Zen: Simple Ideas on Presentation Design and Delivery
Second Edition
Garr Reynolds

New Riders
1249 Eighth Street
Berkeley, CA 94710
510/524-2178
510/524-2221 (fax)

Find us on the Web at: www.newriders.com
To report errors, please send a note to errata@peachpit.com

New Riders is an imprint of Peachpit, a division of Pearson Education

Senior Editor: Karyn Johnson
Copy Editor: Kelly Kordes Anton
Production Editor: Cory Borman
Proofreader: Roxanna Aliaga
Indexer: Emily Glossbrenner
Design Consultant in Japan: Mayumi Nakamoto
Book Cover and Interior Design: Garr Reynolds

ISBN-13: 978-0-321-81198-1
ISBN-10:   0-321-81198-4

9 8 7 6

Printed and bound in the United States of America

To Mom & Dad

Table of Contents

Acknowledgments

This book would not have been possible without a lot of help and support. I'd like to thank the following people for their contributions and encouragement:

Nancy Duarte and Mark Duarte and all the amazing staff at Duarte, Inc. in Silicon Valley, including Nicole Reginelli and Paula Tesch for their constant support.

At New Riders: Michael Nolan who asked me to write this book originally and Karyn Johnson who oversaw the book development this time around and gave me the freedom to do it my way (yeah, like the song). Kelly Kordes Anton and Roxanna Aliaga, for bringing more clarity to my writing and uncovering errors and offering advice for improvement. Mimi Heft for her help with the design and the cover. Hilal Sala, for her great help and guidance in the first edition, and to Cory Borman, for his talent and guidance in production on this edition.

Guy Kawasaki, Seth Godin, David S. Rose, Daniel Pink, Dan Heath and Rick Heath, Rosamund Zander, Jim Quirk, and Deryn Verity for their enlightened advice and content in the early stages of the process.

Jumpei Matsuoka and all the cool people at iStockphoto.com for their tremendous support with the images and the special offer that's included at the back of this book.

Designer Mayumi Nakamoto for teaching me more than I wanted to know (or thought possible) about Adobe InDesign. June Cohen and Michael Glass at TED for their help with the images. Daniel Lee at Mojo for his help with the credits. Aaron Walker, Tom Grant's producer in Japan, for his great assistance.

The Design Matters Japan community including Toru Yamada, Shigeki Yamamoto, Tom Perry, Darren Saunders, Daniel Rodriguez, Kjeld Duits, David Baldwin, Nathan Bryan, Jiri Mestecky, Doug Schafer, Barry Louie, and many, many others.

Back in the States, a big thank you to those who contributed ideas and support, including Debbie Thorn, CZ Robertson, David Roemer, Gail Murphy, Ric Bretschneider, Howard Cooperstein, Dan Roam and Carmine Gallo. And thanks to Mark and Liz Reynolds for their fantastic B&B at the beach.

I'd like to thank the thousands of subscribers to the Presentation Zen blog and to all the blog readers who have contacted me over the years to share their stories and examples, especially Les Posen in Australia.

Although I could not include all the slides in this book, I want to thank all the people who submitted sample slides, including: Jeff Brenman, Chris Landry, Scott B. Schwertly, Jill Cadarette, Kelli Matthews, Luis Iturriaga, Dr. Aisyah Saad Abdul Rahim, Marty Neumeier, Markuz Wernli Saito, Sangeeta Kumar, Allysson Lucca, Pam Slim, Jed Schmidt, Merlin Mann, and many others. Also, a big thank you to Dr. Andreas Eenfeldt in Stockholm and Phil Waknell and Pierre Morsa in Paris.

And, of course, my biggest supporter in all this was my wife, Ai, who was always understanding and a great source of inspiration and ideas (and occasionally, chocolate-chip cookies).

Foreword by Guy Kawasaki

Because this is a book about presenting better with slides, I thought it would be appropriate to show the foreword as a slide presentation. As far as I know, this is the first foreword in history presented in a book as a series of presentation slides. Now, good slides should *enhance* a live talk; slides are not meant to tell the whole story without you there. But from the slides on the next page, I think you can get my point. If I were to give a live talk about why you should buy this book, the slides would look something like this.

Guy Kawasaki
Author of *Enchantment: The Art of Changing Hearts, Minds, and Actions*, and former chief evangelist of Apple
www.guykawasaki.com

introduction

Simplicity is the ultimate sophistication.

— Leonardo da Vinci

Presenting in Today's World

With successful presentations in Tokyo behind me, I boarded the 5:03 p.m. Super Express bound for Osaka complete with my *ekiben* (a special kind of Japanese lunch box or *bento* sold at train stations) and a can of Asahi beer in hand. The quintessential "Japan experience" for me is zipping through the Japanese countryside aboard cutting-edge rail technology while sampling traditional Japanese delicacies with my chopsticks, sipping Japanese beer, and catching glimpses of temples, shrines, and even Mount Fuji outside the spacious side window. It's a wonderful juxtaposition of the old and the new— and a pleasant way to end the day.

While in the midst of savoring the contents of my bento, I glanced across the aisle to see a Japanese businessman with a pensive look on his face as he reviewed a printed deck of PowerPoint slides. Two slides per page, one page after another filled with boxes crammed with reams of Japanese text in several different colors. No empty space. No graphics except for the company logo at the top of each slide box. Just slide after slide of text, subject titles, bullet points, and logos.

Were these slides the visual support for a live oral presentation? If so, I sympathized with the audience. Since when can an audience read and listen to someone talk at the same time (even if they could actually see the 12-point text on the screen well enough to read it)? Were the slides used merely as a kind of document printed in PowerPoint? If so, I pitied both the author and the reader because PowerPoint is not a tool for document creation. Boxes of bullet points and logos do not make for a good handout or report. And judging by the way the man flipped back and forth between the printed slides, perhaps frustrated by the ambiguity of the content, this was becoming apparent to him.

What a contrast in the presentation of content, I thought to myself: The beautifully efficient, well-designed Japanese bento before me containing nothing superfluous, compared with the poorly designed, difficult-to-understand deck of printed PowerPoint slides across the aisle. Why couldn't the design and presentation of business and technical content for a live talk have more in common with the spirit of the simple bentos sold at Japanese train stations? For example, the Japanese bento contains appropriate content arranged in the most efficient, graceful manner. The bento is presented in a simple, beautiful, and balanced way. Nothing lacking. Nothing superfluous. Not decorated, but wonderfully designed. It looks good, and it *is* good. A satisfying, inspiring, and fulfilling way to spend 20 minutes. When was the last time you could say the same about a presentation you saw?

A delicious Japanese bento and a slide presentation may seem to have nothing in common. But it was at that moment, rolling across Japan at 200 miles an hour many years ago, that I had a realization: something needed to be done to end the scourge of bad PowerPoint slides and the lifeless narration that accompanies them—and I could do something to help. In Japan, just like everywhere else in the world, professionals suffer through poorly designed presentations on a daily basis. Presentations in which the slides often do more harm than good. It is not enjoyable, and it is not effective. I knew that if I could begin to help others look at preparation, design, and delivery of so-called "PowerPoint presentations" in a different way, perhaps I could do my small part to help others communicate far more effectively. That moment on the Bullet Train—somewhere between Yokohama and Nagoya—was when I began writing this book. I started by sharing my thoughts on the Presentation Zen website, a blog that would go on to become the world's most visited site on presentation design.

This book has three sections: Preparation, Design, and Delivery. Along the way, I'll provide a good balance of principles and concepts, inspiration, and practical examples. I'll even show you before-and-after photos of the actual bento box that was the inspiration for this book. Before reviewing the current state of presentations today—and why presentations matter now more than ever before—let's first look at what is meant by "Presentation Zen."

The Presentation Zen Approach

This is not a book about Zen. This is a book about communication and about seeing presentations in a slightly different way, a way that is in tune with our times. Although I make several references to Zen and the Zen arts along the way, my references are far more in the realm of an analogy than the literal. Literally, the tradition of Zen or Zen practice has nothing to do directly with the art of presenting in today's world. However, our professional activities—especially professional communications—can share the same ethos as Zen. That is, the essence or the spirit of many principles found in Zen concerning aesthetics, mindfulness, connectedness, and so on can be applied to our daily activities, including presentations.

A teacher for one who seeks enlightenment would say that the first step for the student is to truly see that life is somehow out-of-sync or off-kilter, that there is "suffering" if you will. And that this "out-of-kilterness" is a consequence of our own attachment to things that are inconsequential. Likewise, the first step to creating and designing great presentations is to be mindful of the current state of what passes for "normal" presentations and that what is "normal" today is off-kilter with how people actually learn and communicate.

Each situation is different. But we all know, through our own experiences, that presentations in business and academia can cause a good degree of "suffering" for audiences and presenters alike. If we want to communicate with more clarity, integrity, beauty, and intelligence, then we must move beyond what is considered to be "normal" to something different and far more effective. The principles I am most mindful of through every step of the presentation process are restraint, simplicity, and naturalness: Restraint in preparation. Simplicity in design. Naturalness in delivery. All of which, in the end, lead to greater clarity for us and for our audiences.

In many ways, few of the basics have changed since the time of Aristotle some 2,300 years ago, or from the basic advice given by Dale Carnegie in the 1930s. But what may seem like common sense regarding presentations is not common practice. The Presentation Zen approach challenges the conventional wisdom of making slide presentations in today's world and encourages people to think differently about the design and delivery of their presentations.

An Approach, Not a Method

Presentation Zen is an approach, not a method. Method implies a step-by-step, systematic, planned, and linear process. Method suggests a definite and proven procedure that you can pick off a shelf and follow from A to Z in a logical, orderly fashion. As an approach, Presentation Zen suggests a road, a direction, a frame of mind—perhaps even a philosophy—but not a formula of proven rules to be followed. Methods are important and necessary. But there are no panaceas, and I offer no prescriptions for success. Success depends on you and your own unique situation. However, I do offer guidelines and some things to think about that may run contrary to conventional wisdom on how to make live presentations with multimedia.

Similarly, Zen itself is an approach to life and a way of being rather than a set of rules or dogma to be followed by all in the same way. Indeed, there are many paths to enlightenment. At the heart of Zen is the need for personal awareness and the ability to see and discover. Zen is practical. It's concerned with the here and now. And the practical and the here and now are also our concern with presentations. The aim of this book is to help professionals free themselves from the pain of creating and delivering presentations by helping them see presentations in a way that is different, simpler, more visual, more natural, and ultimately far more meaningful.

Each Case Is Different

Not all presentation situations are appropriate for using multimedia. For example, if you have a small audience and data-intensive materials to discuss, a handout of the materials with a give-and-take discussion is usually more appropriate. In many situations, a whiteboard, flipcharts, or a paper with detailed figures would make for better support. Each case is different. The discussions in this book, however, center on those presentations for which multimedia is a good fit for your unique situation.

This book is not directly about software tools. Yet, by keeping principles such as restraint and simplicity in mind, you can use the lessons here to help you design better visuals that are appropriate to a given situation. When it comes to software functions, I don't think the challenge is to learn more, but rather to ignore more so that you can focus on the principles and the few techniques that are important. Software techniques are simply not our chief concern.

Characterizing master swordsman Odagiri Ichiun's ideas on technique, Zen scholar Daisetz T. Suzuki says, "The first principle of the art is not to rely on tricks of technique. Most swordsmen make too much of technique, sometimes making it their chief concern." Most presenters, however, make the software their chief concern in the preparation process and delivery. This often produces cluttered visuals and talks that are neither engaging nor memorable.

Yes, the basics of software are important to know. Delivery techniques and "do's and dont's" are useful to understand. But it's not about technique alone. The "art of presentation" transcends technique and enables an individual to remove walls and connect with an audience— to inform or persuade in a very meaningful, unique moment in time.

Presentations Today

It seems that computer-generated slide presentations have been around forever, but in truth they've only been in common use for about 20 to 25 years. PowerPoint 1.0 was created in Silicon Valley in 1987 by Robert Gaskins and Dennis Austin as a way to display presentations on a Mac. It was cool. And it worked. They sold the application later that year to Microsoft. A version for Windows hit the market a couple years later, and (oy vey!) the world hasn't been the same since. As popular author Seth Godin—who's seen more bad presentations than any man should be subjected to—says in his 2001 e-book *Really Bad PowerPoint* (the best-selling e-book of that year): "PowerPoint could be the most powerful tool on your computer, but it's not. It's actually a dismal failure. Almost every PowerPoint presentation sucks rotten eggs."

Over the years, a primary reason so many presentations given with the aid of slides or other multimedia have failed is that the visual displays served as nothing more than containers for reams of text. According to John Sweller, who developed the cognitive load theory in the 1980s, it is more difficult to process information if it is coming at us both verbally and in written form at the same time. Since people cannot read and listen well at the same time, displays filled with lots of text must be avoided. On the other hand, multimedia that displays visual information, including visualizations of quantitative information, *can* be processed while listening to someone speak about the visual content.

Most of us know intuitively that when given 20 minutes to present, using screens full of text does not work. Research supports the concept that it is indeed more difficult for audiences to process information when it is presented in spoken and written form at the same time. So perhaps it would be better to just remain silent and let people read the slides. But this raises the issue: Why are you there? A good oral presentation is different from a well-written document, and attempts to merge them result in poor presentations and poor documents, as I explain later in this book.

Still a Long Way to Go

While presentation technology has evolved over the years, the presentations themselves have not necessarily evolved. Today, millions of presentations are given every day with the aid of desktop applications such as PowerPoint and Keynote, and cloud-based applications such as Google Docs and Prezi. Yet, most presentations remain mind-numbingly dull, something to be endured by both presenter and audience alike, or heavily decorated and animated affairs with excessive motion that distracts from even well-researched content. Presentations are still generally ineffective, not because presenters lack intelligence or creativity, but because they have learned bad habits and they lack awareness and knowledge about what makes for a great presentation.

Although presentation techniques have changed as digital technology has progressed, the fundamentals of what makes an effective presentation today are essentially the same as they ever were. The principles of restraint, simplicity, and naturalness are still key, regardless of what software you use—and even if you use no digital tools at all. And no matter how much we use software in a live presentation, as much as possible the tools and techniques must be used only to clarify, simplify, and support the personal connection that develops between an audience and a speaker. The latest tools and technology can be great enablers and amplifiers of our messages, but they must be used wisely and with restraint in a way that feels natural and real, otherwise they become barriers to communication.

No matter how impressive technology becomes in the future, no matter how many features and effects are added, the technology of the soul has not changed. Technologies such as PowerPoint and Keynote—and new tools such as Prezi—are only useful to the degree that they make things clearer and more memorable, and strengthen the human-to-human connection that is the basis of communication. Used well, multimedia has the power to do this.

Presentation Generation

The ability to stand and deliver a powerful presentation that engages each audience member's whole mind has never been more important than today. Some have called our modern era the "presentation generation." One reason that the ability to speak passionately, clearly, and visually is more important today than ever before is the fantastic reach our talks can have, largely thanks to the power of online video. What you say and what you present visually can now be captured easily and cheaply in HD video and broadcast around the world for anyone to see. The potential of your speech or presentation to change things—maybe even change the world—goes far beyond just the words spoken. Words are important; but if it was just about words, we could create a detailed document, disseminate it, and that would be that. An effective presentation allows us to amplify the meaning of our words.

While speaking about the power of online video to spread innovative ideas at the TED Global conference in Oxford, England, in 2010, TED Curator Chris Anderson spoke of the great power of face-to-face communication and presentations to influence change. Anderson underscored the fact that information usually can be taken in faster by reading—but a necessary depth and richness is often missing. Part of the effectiveness of a presentation is the visual impact and the show-and-tell aspect of it. The presentation visuals, the structure, and the story are compelling aspects of a presentation, even a recorded presentation that is put up on the Web. However, as Anderson says, there is much more to it than that:

> "*There's a lot more being transferred than just words. It is in that nonverbal portion that there's some serious magic. Somewhere hidden in the physical gestures, the vocal cadence, the facial expressions, the eye contact, the passion.... There are hundreds of subconscious clues that go to how well you will understand and whether you are inspired.*"

We are wired for face-to-face communication, Anderson says. "Face-to-face communication has been fine tuned by millions of years of evolution. That's what's made it into this mysterious powerful thing it is. Someone speaks, and there is resonance in all these receiving brains. [Then] the whole group acts together. This is the connective tissue of the human super organism in action. It has driven our culture for millennia."

Raising the Bar and Making a Difference

Organizations such as TED have proven that well-crafted and engaging presentations can teach, persuade, and inspire. Progress is being made on the presentation front. However, on the whole, the majority of presentations in business and academia are still tedious affairs that fail to engage audiences, even though the content may be important.

The bar is still relatively low when it comes to the quality of presentations, especially those given with the aid of multimedia. But this is not necessarily bad news—in fact, it is an opportunity. It's an opportunity for you to be different. You have important ideas that are worth sharing, so now is not the time to hesitate. If you look at the really successful and innovative companies and organizations around the world today, they are often the ones that celebrate individual and creative contributions. In that spirit, presenting your work and your great ideas is no time to be timid. Life is too short. If you want to change things—including the arc of your own career—then how you present yourself and your ideas matters a great deal. Why not be different?

TED and TEDx events demonstrate the power of clear, meaningful, and visual presentations.
(Photo: TEDxTokyo/Andy McGovern.)

Presentations in the "Conceptual Age"

One of my favorite books is Daniel Pink's best-seller, *A Whole New Mind* (Riverhead Trade). Tom Peters called the book "a miracle." There's a reason. *A Whole New Mind* gives context to the Presentation Zen approach to presenting in today's world, an era that Pink and others have dubbed the "Conceptual Age," where "high-touch" and "high-concept" aptitudes are first among equals. "The future belongs to a different kind of person," Pink says. "Designers, inventors, teachers, storytellers—creative and empathetic right-brain thinkers whose abilities mark the fault line between who gets ahead and who doesn't."

In *A Whole New Mind,* Pink paints an accurate and vivid picture of the threats and opportunities facing professionals today. Pink claims we're living in a different era, a different age. This is an age in which those who "think different" will be valued even more than ever. According to Pink, we're living in an age that is "animated by a different form of thinking and a new approach to life—one that prizes aptitudes that I call 'high concept' and 'high touch.' High concept involves the capacity to detect patterns and opportunities, to create artistic and emotional beauty, to craft a satisfying narrative...."

Now, Pink is not saying that logic and analysis ("left-brain reasoning"), which are so important in the Information Age, are not important in the Conceptual Age of today. Indeed, logical thinking is as important as it ever has been. "Right-brain reasoning" alone is not going to keep a space shuttle up or cure disease. Logical reasoning is a necessary condition. However, it's increasingly clear that logic alone is not a sufficient condition for success for individuals and organizations. Right-brain thinking is every bit as important now—in some cases, more important—than left-brain thinking. (The right-brain/left-brain distinction is a metaphor based on real differences between the two hemispheres; a healthy person uses both hemispheres for even simple tasks.)

Particularly valuable in *A Whole New Mind* are the "six senses" or the six "right-brain directed aptitudes," which Pink says are necessary for successful professionals to possess in the more interdependent world we live in, a world of increased automation and outsourcing.

The six aptitudes are: design, story, symphony, empathy, play, and meaning. Mastering these aptitudes is not sufficient; leveraging these aptitudes has become necessary for professional success and personal fulfillment in today's world. The introduction to the aptitudes that follows is written with multimedia-enhanced presentations in mind. But, you could take the six aptitudes and apply them to the art of game design, programming, product design, project management, health care, teaching, retail, and so on. The slide below summarizes six of the key points found in Pink's book.

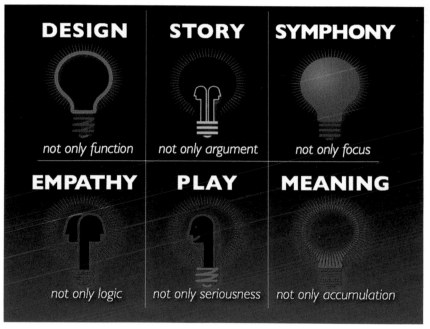

(The original images in the slide are from a vector file from iStockphoto.com, file no. 700018.)

Design

To many business people, design is something you spread on the surface, like icing on a cake. It's nice, but not mission critical. This is not design to me—it's decoration. Decoration, for better or worse, is noticeable. It is sometimes enjoyable and sometimes irritating, and it is unmistakably there. The best designs, however, are so well done that the observer never even consciously notices the design. Think about the design of a book or the signage in an airport. We take note of the messages that the design helped make utterly clear, but not the color palette, typography, concept, etc.

Design starts at the beginning, not at the end—it's not an afterthought. If you use slideware in your presentation, the design of the visuals needs to begin in the preparation stage, before you even turn on your computer. During the preparation stage, you slow down and "stop your busy mind" so you can consider your topic, objectives, key messages, and audience. Only then will you begin to sketch out ideas that will appear in some digital visual form.

Story

Facts, information, data. Most of it is available online or can be sent to people via e-mail, PDF, or hard copy through snail mail. Data and fact have never been more widely available. Cognitive scientist Mark Turner calls storytelling "narrative imagining," something that is a key instrument of thought. We are wired to tell and receive stories. We are all born storytellers (and "storylisteners"). As kids, we looked forward to show-and-tell, and we gathered with our friends at recess and lunchtime to tell stories about real things and real events that mattered, at least to us.

But somewhere along the line, "story" became synonymous with fiction or even falsehood. So story and storytelling have been marginalized in business and academia as something serious people do not engage in. But, from what college students tell me, I've concluded that the best and most effective professors are the ones who tell true stories. From my students' point of view, the best professors don't just go through the material in a book. They put their own personality, character, and experiences into the material in the form of a narrative, which is illuminating, engaging, and memorable. Stories can be used for good—for teaching, sharing, illuminating, and, of course, honest persuasion.

Symphony

Focus, specialization, and analysis have been important in the Information Age, but in the Conceptual Age, the ability to synthesize seemingly unrelated pieces to form and articulate the big picture is crucial—even a differentiator. Pink calls this aptitude "symphony."

The best presenters can illuminate relationships we may not have seen before. They can see the relationships between relationships. Symphony requires that we become better at seeing—truly seeing—in a new way. Anyone can deliver chunks of information and repeat findings that are represented visually by bullet points on screen. What we need are people who can recognize the patterns and are skilled at seeing the nuances and simplicity that may exist in a complex problem. Symphony in the world of presentation does not mean dumbing down information into the sound bites and talking points so popular in the mass media. Symphony is about applying our whole mind—logic, analysis, synthesis, intuition—to make sense of our world (that is, our topic), find the big picture, and determine what is important and what is not before the day of a talk. It's also about deciding what matters and letting go of the rest.

Empathy

Empathy is emotional. It's about putting yourself in the position of others. It involves an understanding of the importance of others' nonverbal cues and being aware of your own. Good designers, for example, have the ability to put themselves in the position of the user, customer, or audience member. This is a talent, perhaps, more than a skill that can be taught—but everyone can get better at it. Empathy allows a presenter, even without thinking about it, to notice when the audience is "getting it" and when they are not. The empathetic presenter can make adjustments based on his or her reading of a particular audience.

Play

In the Conceptual Age, says Pink, work is not just about seriousness, but about play as well. While each presentation situation is different, in many public speaking situations playfulness and humor can go a long way toward making a presentation palatable. Humor, in this sense, does not imply joking or clown-like informality, but rather, good, old-fashioned humor that leads to laughter. In Pink's book, Indian physician Madan Kataria points out that many think serious people are the best suited for business—that serious people are more responsible: "[But] that's not true. That's yesterday's news. Laughing people are more creative people. They are more productive people."

Somewhere along the line, we were sold the idea that a real business presentation or academic talk must be dull and devoid of humor—something to be endured, not enjoyed. And if you use multimedia tools, the more complicated, detailed, and difficult to see, the better. This approach is still alive and well today, but we can hope in the future that this, too, will become "yesterday's news."

TEDxTokyo Curator Patrick Newell plays with the audience on stage between presentations.
(Photo: TEDxTokyo/Andy McGovern.)

Meaning

Making a presentation is an opportunity to make a small difference in the world, whether it's in your community, company, or school. A presentation that goes badly may have a devastating impact on your spirit (and on your career). But a presentation that goes well can be extremely fulfilling for both you and the audience, and it might even help your career. Some say that we "are born for meaning." We live for self-expression and an opportunity to share what we believe is important. If you are lucky, you're in a job that you feel passionate about. If so, then it's with excitement that you look forward to the possibility of sharing your expertise—your story—with others. Few things can be more rewarding than connecting with someone by teaching something new or sharing something you believe is very important with others.

Audiences are so used to death-by-PowerPoint that they've seemingly learned to see it as normal, even if not ideal. However, if you are different—if you exceed expectations, show the audience that you've thought about them, done your homework, know your material, and demonstrated through your actions how much you appreciate being there—chances are you'll make an impact and a difference, even if it's just in the smallest of ways. There can be great meaning in even these small connections.

Design. Story. Symphony. Empathy. Play. Meaning. Dan Pink's *A Whole New Mind* gives us the context of the new world we're living in and explains why "high-touch" talents—which include exceptional presentation skills— are so important today. Professionals around the globe need to understand how and why the right-brain aptitudes of design, story, symphony, empathy, play, and meaning are more important than ever. The best presentations of our generation will be created by professionals—engineers as well as CEOs and creative types—who have strong "whole mind" aptitudes and talents. These are not the only aptitudes needed by the modern presenter, but mastering these talents along with other important abilities (such as strong analytical skills) will take you far as a communicator in the Conceptual Age.

Seth Godin

Speaker, blogger, and author of *We Are All Weird*
www.sethgodin.com

Marketing guru and presenter extraordinaire Seth Godin says presentation is about the transfer of emotion.

It doesn't matter whether you're trying to champion at a church or a school or a Fortune 100 company, you're probably going to use PowerPoint. PowerPoint was developed by engineers as a tool to help them communicate with the marketing department—and vice versa. It's a remarkable tool because it allows very dense verbal communication. Yes, you could send a memo, but no one reads anymore. As our companies are getting faster and faster, we need a way to communicate ideas from one group to another. Enter PowerPoint.

PowerPoint could be the most powerful tool on your computer. But it's not. Countless innovations fail because their champions use PowerPoint the way Microsoft wants them to, instead of the right way.

Communication is about getting others to adopt your point of view, to help them understand why you're excited (or sad, or optimistic, or whatever else you are). If all you want to do is create a file of facts and figures, then cancel the meeting and send in a report.

Our brains have two sides. The right side is emotional, musical, and moody. The left side is focused on dexterity, facts, and hard data. When you show up to give a presentation, people want to use both parts of their brains. So they use the right side to judge the way you talk, the way you dress, and your body language. Often, people come to a conclusion about your presentation by the time you're on the second slide. After that, it's often too late for your bullet points to do you much good. You can wreck a communication process with lousy logic or unsupported facts, but you can't complete it without emotion. Logic is not enough. Communication is the transfer of emotion.

Champions must sell—to internal audiences and to the outside world. If everyone in the room agreed with you, you wouldn't need to do a presentation, would you? You could save a lot of time by printing out a one-page project report and delivering it to each person. No, the reason we do presentations is to make a point, to sell one or more ideas.

If you believe in your idea, sell it. Make your point as hard as you can and get what you came for. Your audience will thank you for it, because deep down, we all want to be sold.

How to Improve Immediately

First, make slides that reinforce your words, not repeat them. Create slides that demonstrate, with emotional proof, that what you're saying is true, not just accurate. No more than six words on a slide. EVER. There is no presentation so complex that this rule needs to be broken.

Second, don't use cheesy images. Use professional stock photo images. Talking about pollution in Houston? Instead of giving me four bullet points of EPA data, why not read me the stats but show me a photo of a bunch of dead birds, some smog, and even a diseased lung? This is cheating! It's unfair! It works.

Third, no dissolves, spins, or other transitions. Keep it simple.

Fourth, create a written document. A leave-behind. Put in as many footnotes or details as you like. Then, when you start your presentation, tell the audience that you're going to give them all the details of your presentation after it's over, and they don't have to write down everything you say. Remember, the presentation is to make an emotional sale. The document is the proof that helps the intellectuals in your audience accept the idea that you've sold them on emotionally. Don't hand out printouts of your slides. They don't work without you there.

The home run is easy to describe: You put up a slide. It triggers an emotional reaction in the audience. They sit up and want to know what you're going to say that fits in with that image. Then, if you do it right, every time they think of what you said, they'll see the image (and vice versa). Sure, this is different from the way everyone else does it. But everyone else is busy defending the status quo (which is easy) and you're busy championing brave new innovations, which is difficult.

Lyza Danger Gardner

Sample Slides

Here are a few sample slides from one of Seth's presentations. Without Seth, these visuals are almost meaningless. But with Seth's engaging narrative, the visuals help illuminate a memorable story.

A New Era Requires New Thinking

The skills necessary to be an effective communicator today are different than in the past. Today, literacy is not only about reading and writing—which are necessary—but also about understanding visual communication. Today, we need a higher degree of visual literacy and an understanding of the great power that imagery has for conveying important messages.

People who design visuals for live presentations typically regard PowerPoint as a kind of document-creation tool. Their principles and techniques seem to be largely influenced by the conventional wisdom regarding the proper creation of business documents such as letters, reports, spreadsheets, and so on. Many businesspeople and students approach multimedia slides as if they were nothing more than glorified overhead transparencies that contain boxes for text, bullets, and clip art.

If you want to learn how to become a better presenter, then look beyond the advice given in books about how to use PowerPoint and books on presentation skills (including this one). These books have their place, but you should be looking to other forms of proven visual storytelling as well. Documentary films, for example, tell nonfiction stories that incorporate narration, interviews, audio, powerful video and still images, and at times, on-screen text. These elements can be incorporated into live oral presentations as well. Cinema and presentations are different, but not as different as you may think. I have learned much about the use of imagery in storytelling from watching virtually every documentary Ken Burns ever produced. And there are useful lessons in storytelling and visual communication found in great films such as *Citizen Kane, Casablanca,* Kurosawa's *Ikiru,* and even the *Star Wars* trilogy.

The art of comics is another place to look for knowledge and inspiration. Comics, for example, are amazingly effective at partnering text and images to form a powerful narrative that is engaging and memorable.

Comics and film are two major ways stories are told through imagery. The principles and techniques for creating a presentation for a conference or a keynote address have more in common with the principles and techniques behind the creation of a good documentary film or a good comic book than the creation of a conventional static business document with bullet points.

Letting Go

Part of the Presentation Zen approach to presenting well is learning to give up what you've learned about making presentations in the PowerPoint era with its cookie-cutter method of design and delivery. The first step is to stop allowing our history and conditioning about what we know—or thought we knew—to keep us from being open to other ways of presentation. Seven sentences per slide? Some clip art thrown in for good measure? No one ever got fired for that, right? But if we remain attached to the past, we cannot learn anything new. We must open our minds so that we can see the world for what it is with a fresh new perspective. As the great Master Yoda once suggested (in a galaxy far, far away), we must unlearn what we have learned.

(*Image in this slide from iStockphoto.com.*)

EXERCISE

Hold a brainstorming session, alone or with your workgroup, to examine any current views and guidelines you have concerning your organization's presentations. How are your current presentations off-kilter? In what ways are they in sync? What questions should you be asking about presentation design and delivery that you have not asked in the past? What aspects of the design and delivery process have caused "suffering" for your presenters and your audiences? Have past efforts been focused too much on the inconsequential things? What are the "inconsequential" aspects and where can the focus shift?

In Sum

- Like a Japanese bento, great slide presentations contain appropriate content arranged in the most efficient, graceful manner without superfluous decoration. The presentation of the content is simple, balanced, and beautiful.

- Presentation Zen is an approach, not an inflexible list of rules to be followed by all in the same way. There are many paths to designing and delivering presentations.

- The key principles of Presentation Zen are: Restraint in preparation. Simplicity in design. Naturalness in delivery. These principles can be applied to both technical and nontechnical presentations.

- The dull, text-filled slide approach is common and normal, but it is not effective. The problem is not one of tools or technique—it is a problem of bad habits. While some tools are better than others, it is possible to present effectively with the aid of multimedia tools.

- In the Conceptual Age, solid presentation skills are more important than ever before. Presenting well is a "whole-mind" skill. Good presenters target people's left brain and right brain sensibilities.

- Live talks enhanced by multimedia are about storytelling and have more in common with the art of documentary film than the reading of a paper document. Live talks today must tell a story enhanced by imagery and other forms of appropriate multimedia.

- We've learned some ineffective habits over the years. The first step to change is letting go of the past.

Such power there is in clear-eyed self-restraint.

— James Russell

Creativity, Limitations, and Constraints

In Chapter 3, we take a look at the first steps in the preparation stage. But first, let's take a step back and look at something we usually do not think about when preparing a presentation: creativity. You may not think of yourself as being creative, let alone as a creative professional like a designer, writer, artist, and so on. But developing presentation content—especially content to be delivered with the aid of multimedia—is a creative act.

Most of the students and professionals I meet in classes and seminars around the world say that they are "not very creative." Some of this is modesty no doubt, but I think most adults genuinely believe this. They have convinced themselves that creative is just not a term they would use to describe themselves. And yet these are adults who do well in their jobs and generally have happy and productive lives. How is it that they believe they are not creative or that their jobs do not require high levels of creativity? On the other hand, if you ask a room full of young children if they are creative, you'll see just about every hand go up. Pablo Picasso said that "all children are born artists, the problem is to remain an artist as we grow up." The same can be said for creativity. You were born creative and you still are that creative being today, no matter what your career path. There are many ways to express your creativity, and designing and delivering an effective presentation is one way to do so.

Creating presentations is a supremely creative process—or it should be. It's as much "right brain" as it is "left brain," and design does matter. Who said that business and creativity were mutually exclusive? Is business only about managing numbers and administration? Can't students become better business leaders tomorrow by learning how to become better design thinkers today? Aren't design thinking, design mindfulness, and creative thinking

valuable aptitudes for all professionals, regardless of their discipline or particular task at hand?

Once you realize that preparing a presentation is an act requiring creativity—not merely the assembling of facts and data in a linear fashion—you'll see that preparing a presentation is a "whole-minded" activity that requires as much right-brain thinking as it does left-brain thinking. In fact, while your research and background work may have required much logical analysis, calculation, and careful evidence gathering using left-brain thinking, the transformation of your content into presentation form will require that you exercise much more of your right brain.

Start with the Beginner's Mind

Zen teachings often speak of the "beginner's mind" or "child's mind." Like a child, one who approaches life with a beginner's mind is fresh, enthusiastic, and open to the vast possibilities of ideas and solutions before them. A child does not know what is not possible and so is open to exploration, discovery, and experimentation. If you approach creative tasks with the beginner's mind, you can see things more clearly, unburdened by your fixed views, habits, and what conventional wisdom says it is (or should be). One who possesses a beginner's mind is not burdened by old habits or obsessed about "the way things are done around here" or with the way things could have or should have been done. A beginner is open, receptive, and more inclined to say "Why not?" or "Let's give it a shot," rather than "It's never been done" or "That's not common."

When you approach a new challenge as a true beginner (even as a seasoned adult), you need not be saddled with fear of failure or making mistakes. If you approach problems with the "expert's mind," you are often blind to the possibilities. Your expert's mind is bound by the past; it is not interested in the new, different, and untried. Your expert's mind will say, "It can't be done" or "It shouldn't be done." Your beginner's mind will say, "I wonder if this can be done?"

If you approach a task with the beginner's mind, you are not afraid of being wrong. The fear of making a mistake, risking an error, or being told you are wrong is constantly with us. And that's a shame. Making mistakes is not the same thing as being creative, but if you are not willing to make mistakes, then it is impossible to be truly creative. If your state of mind is coming from a place of fear and risk avoidance, then you will always settle for the safe solutions—the solutions already applied many times before. And sometimes, the "path already taken" is the best solution. But you should not follow the path automatically without first seeing it for what it really is. When you are open to possibilities, you may find that the most common way is the best way for your particular case. However, this will not be a choice made by habit. You will choose based on reflection and in the spirit of a beginner with fresh eyes and a new perspective.

Children are naturally creative, playful, and experimental. If you ask me, we were the most human when we were young kids. We "worked" on our art, sometimes for hours without a break, because it was in us, although we didn't intellectualize it. As we got older, fears crept in along with doubts, self-censoring, and overthinking. The creative spirit is in us now; it's who we are. We just need to look at the kids around us to be reminded of that. Whether you are 28 or 88, it's never too late, because the child is still in you.

"In the beginner's mind there are many possibilities, in the expert's mind there are few."

—*Shunryu Suzuki*

You Are Creative

Creative power and creative imagination are not only for the artists of the world—painters, sculptors, and so on. Teachers also need the power of creativity. So do programmers, engineers, scientists, etc. You can see the application of creative genius in many professional fields. Remember, it was a group of brilliant and geeky-to-the-core, left-brain NASA engineers on the ground who were able to jury-rig a solution to the life-threatening buildup of carbon dioxide in the damaged Apollo 13 spacecraft back in 1970. Their heroic fix—literally involving duct tape and spare parts—was ingenious improvisation; it was imaginative and creative.

Being creative does not mean wearing a black turtleneck and hanging out in jazz cafés sipping cappuccinos. It means using your whole mind to find solutions. Creativity means not being paralyzed by your methods and knowledge, but being able to think outside the box (sometimes very quickly) to find solutions to unforeseen problems. This kind of situation requires logic and analysis, but also big-picture thinking. And big-picture thinking is a right-brain, creative aptitude.

Back down here on earth, the seemingly mundane business of a conference presentation, designed and delivered with the help of slideware, can be a very creative thing. A presentation is an opportunity to differentiate yourself, your organization, or your cause. It's your chance to tell the story of why your content is important and why it matters. It can be an opportunity to make a difference. So why look or talk like everyone else? Why strive to meet expectations? Why not surpass expectations and surprise people?

You are a creative person—probably far more creative than you think. All people should work toward tapping into their creative abilities and unleashing their imaginations. *If You Want to Write* by Brenda Ueland (Graywolf Press) is one of the most inspiring and useful books I have ever read. The book was first published in 1938 and probably should have been titled "If You Want to Be Creative." Her simple yet sage advice will be of interest not only to writers but to anyone who yearns to be more creative in their work or to help others get in touch with their creative souls (this goes for programmers and epidemiologists, as well as designers and artists). This book should be required reading for all professionals and especially those aspiring to teach anyone about anything. Following are ideas inspired by Brenda Ueland that you should keep in mind when preparing for a presentation or any other creative endeavor in your work.

The Big Lie

Ah, the big lie we tell ourselves: "I am not creative." Sure, you might not be the next Picasso in your field. (Then again, who knows?) But it doesn't matter. What matters is to not close yourself down too early in the exploration process. Failing is fine; it's necessary, in fact. But avoiding experimentation or risk—especially out of fear of what others may think—is something that will gnaw at your gut more than any ephemeral failure. A failure is in the past. It's done and over. But worrying about "what might be if..." or "what might have been if I had..." are pieces of baggage you carry around daily. They're heavy, and they'll kill your creative spirit. Take chances and stretch yourself. You're only here on this planet once, and for a very short time at that. Why not just see how gifted you are? You may surprise someone. Most importantly, you may surprise yourself.

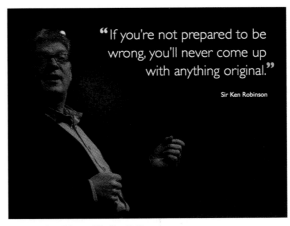

Image in this slide is of Sir Ken Robinson presenting at TED in 2006. (Original photo courtesy of TED/ leslieimage.com.)

Be a Pirate!

Inspiration. Where can you find it? You can find inspiration in a million places, in a million ways—but probably not in your same old routine. Sometimes, you can find inspiration in teaching. When you teach someone something important to you, you are reminded of why it matters, and the enthusiasm of the student—child or adult—is infectious and energizing. Ueland says, "I helped them by trying to make them feel freer, bolder. Let her go! Be careless, reckless! Be a lion. Be a pirate!" You know it's important to be free, free like children are. You just need to be reminded of that occasionally.

Do Not Force It

Idling—doing nothing—is important. Most of us, myself included, are obsessed with getting things done. We're afraid to be unproductive. And yet, the big ideas often come during your periods of "laziness," during those episodes of "wasting time." People need more time away from the direct challenges of work. Taking long walks on the beach, jogging through the forest, going for bike rides, reading the Sunday paper for four to five hours in a coffee shop. During these times, your creative spirit is energized. Sometimes you need solitude and a break to slow down so that you may see things differently. Managers who understand this and give their staff the time they need (which they can only do by genuinely trusting them) are the secure managers—and the best managers.

Enthusiasm

Put your love, passion, imagination, and spirit behind it. Without enthusiasm, there is no creativity. It may be a quiet enthusiasm, or it may be loud. It doesn't matter, as long as it is real. I remember a guy's comment on a successful long-term project of mine: "Well, you have enthusiasm, I'll give you that." He didn't realize that it was a backhanded compliment. These are the people who get us down. Life is short. Don't hang out with people who dismiss the idea of enthusiasm, or worse still, with those who try to kill yours. Trying to impress others or worrying about what others may think of your enthusiasm or passion should be the last thing on your mind.

When forced to work within a strict framework the imagination is taxed to its utmost—and will produce its richest ideas. Given total freedom the work is likely to sprawl.

—T.S. Eliot

The Art of Working with Restrictions

My friends at Universal Studios Japan—Jasper von Meerheimb, senior art director, and Sachiko Kawamura, senior environmental graphic designer—gave an excellent presentation for Design Matters Japan on the issue of how restrictive conditions put on creative projects can lead to inventive solutions. In their presentation, they talked about how to develop concepts and implement them under constraints such as limited time, space, and budgets. For professional designers, creating great work under a thousand constraints and limitations imposed from the outside is simply the way the world of design works. Whether constraints are good or bad, enabling or crippling, is in a sense irrelevant; constraints are the way of the world. Still, as John Maeda points out in *The Laws of Simplicity* (MIT Press), "In the field of design there is the belief that with more constraints, better solutions are revealed." Time, for example, and the sense of urgency that it brings, is almost always a constraint, yet "urgency and the creative spirit go hand in hand," says Maeda.

Using creativity and skill to solve a problem or design a message among a plethora of restrictions from the client, the boss, and so on, is old hat to designers. They live it. Daily. However, for the millions of nondesigners with access to powerful design tools, the importance of constraints and limitations is not well understood. For those not trained in design, the task of creating presentation visuals (or posters, websites, newsletters, etc.) with today's software tools can make users frustrated by the abundance of options or giddy in anticipation of applying their artistic sensibilities to decorate their work with an ever-increasing array of colors, shapes, and special effects. Either condition can lead to designs and messages that suffer. What you can learn from professional designers is that (1) constraints and limitations are a powerful ally, not an enemy, and (2) creating your own self-imposed constraints, limitations, and parameters is often fundamental to good, creative work.

Self-imposed constraints can help you formulate clearer messages, including visual messages. In the various Zen arts, for example, you'll find that careful study, practice, and adherence to strict guidelines (constraints)

Pecha Kucha: A Sign of the Changing Times

Pecha Kucha is a global presentation phenomenon started in 2003 by Tokyo-based expatriate architects Mark Dytham and Astrid Klein. (*Pecha kucha* is Japanese for "chatter.") Pecha Kucha is an example of the changing attitudes toward presentation and a wonderfully creative and un-conventional way to "do PowerPoint." The Pecha Kucha method of presentation design and delivery is very simple. You must use 20 slides, each shown for 20 seconds, as you tell your story in sync with the visuals. That's 6 minutes and 40 seconds. Slides advance automatically, and when you're done you're done. That's it. Sit down. The objective of these simple but tight restraints is to keep the presentations brief and focused and to give more people a chance to present in a single night.

PechaKucha Nights are held in more than 80 cities from Amsterdam and Auckland to Venice and Vienna. The PechaKucha Nights in Tokyo are hosted in a hip multimedia space, and the atmosphere on the night I attended was a cross between a cool user group meeting and a popular night club.

If nothing else, the Pecha Kucha method is good training and good practice. Everyone should try Pecha Kucha—it's a good exercise for getting your story down even if you do not use this exact method for your own live talk. It doesn't matter whether you can replicate the Pecha Kucha 20 x 20 6:40 method in your own company or school; the spirit behind it and the concept of "restrictions as liberators" can be applied to almost any presentation situation.

This method makes going deep difficult. But if a good discussion arises from a Pecha Kucha type of presentation, then it may work well even inside an organization. I can envision having college students give this kind of presentation about their research followed by deeper questioning and probing by the instructor and class. Which would be more difficult for a student and a better indication of their knowledge: a 45-minute recycled and typical PowerPoint presentation, or a tight 6:40 presentation followed by 30 minutes of probing questions and discussion? On the other hand, if you can't tell the essence of your story in less than seven minutes, then you probably shouldn't be presenting anyway.

Check out the PechaKucha website to find a PechaKucha Night near you.

www.pecha-kucha.org

serve to bring out the creative energy of the individual. For example, haiku has a long tradition and strict guidelines, yet with much practice one can create a message (in 17 syllables or less) that captures both the details and the essence of a moment. The form of haiku may have strict rules, but the rules are what can help you express your own "haiku moments" with both subtlety and depth. In *Wabi Sabi Simple* (Adams Media Corporation, 2004), author Richard Powell comments on wabi sabi, discipline, and simplicity as they relate to such arts as bonsai and haiku:

> *"Do only what is necessary to convey what is essential. [C]arefully eliminate elements that distract from the essential whole, elements that obstruct and obscure.... Clutter, bulk, and erudition confuse perception and stifle comprehension, whereas simplicity allows clear and direct attention."*

Life is about living with limitations of one type or another, but constraints are not necessarily bad. In fact, constraints are helpful, even inspiring as they challenge us to think differently and more creatively about a particular problem. While problems such as a sudden request to give a 20-minute sales pitch or a 45-minute overview of research findings have built-in limitations—such as time, tools, and budget—we can increase our effectiveness by stepping back and thinking long and hard. We can also determine ways to set our own parameters and constraints as we prepare and design our next presentation with greater clarity, focus, balance, and purpose.

As daily life becomes even more complex, and the options and choices continue to mount, crafting messages and making designs that are clear, simple, and concise becomes all the more important. Clarity and simplicity are often all people want or need—yet it's increasingly rare and all the more appreciated when it's discovered. You want to surprise people? You want to exceed their expectations? Then consider making it beautiful, simple, clear... and great. The "greatness" may just be found in what you left out, not in what you left in. It takes creativity and the courage to be different. Your audience is praying that you'll be both creative and courageous.

In Sum

- Preparing, designing, and delivering a presentation is a creative act, and you are a creative being.

- Creativity requires an open mind and a willingness to be wrong.

- Restrictions and limitations are not the enemy; they are a great ally.

- As you prepare a presentation, exercise restraint and always keep these three words in mind: simplicity, clarity, brevity.

3

Planning Analog

One of the most important things you can do in the initial stage of preparing for your presentation is to get away from your computer. A fundamental mistake people make is spending almost the entire time thinking about their talk and preparing their content while sitting in front of a computer screen. Before you design your presentation, you need to see the big picture and identify a single core message or messages. This can be difficult unless you create a stillness of mind for yourself, something that is hard to do while puttering around in slideware.

Right from the start, most people plan their presentations using software tools. In fact, the software makers encourage this, but I don't recommend it. There's just something about using paper and pen to sketch out rough ideas in the "analog world" that seems to lead to more clarity and better, more creative results when we finally get down to representing ideas digitally. Because your presentation will be accompanied by multimedia, you will be spending plenty of time in front of a computer later. I call preparing the presentation away from the computer "going analog," as opposed to "going digital" at the computer.

A Bike or a Car?

Software companies have oversold us on the idea of following templates and wizards, which while sometimes useful, often take us places we do not really want to go. In this sense, visual design expert Edward Tufte is right when he says there is a cognitive style to PowerPoint that leads to an oversimplification of our content and obfuscation of our message. The same could be said of other presentation apps as well. Presentation software applications are wonderful for displaying media in support of our talk, but if we are not careful, these applications also point us down a road that we may not have gone, introducing bells and whistles that may distract more than they help.

More than 25 years ago, Steve Jobs and others in Silicon Valley were talking about the great potential of personal computers and how these tools should be designed and used in a way that enhanced the great potential that exists within each of us. Here's what Steve Jobs said back then in a documentary called *Memory and Imagination* (Michael Lawrence Films):

"What a computer is to me is that it's the most remarkable tool that we've ever come up with, and it's the equivalent of a bicycle for our minds."

— Steve Jobs

When it comes to locomotion, humans are not such an efficient animal compared to other animals. But a human on a bicycle is the most efficient animal on the planet. The bicycle amplifies our input in an enormously productive way. Isn't this what a computer—the most magnificent tool of our time—should do?

During the planning stages of a presentation, does your computer function as a "bicycle for your mind," amplifying your own capabilities and ideas? Or is it more like a "car for your mind" with prepackaged formulas that make your ideas soft? Your mind benefits when you use the computer like a bike, but it loses out when you rely only on your computer's power the way you rely on your car's power.

It's important to understand the principles of presentation creation and design, and not merely follow software application rules. The best software, in many cases, does not so much point the way as it gets out of the way, helping us to amplify our own ideas and abilities. One way to ensure that your computer and your software applications remain great tools of amplification for your ideas and your presentation is to first turn off the computer and walk away from it. You'll be back soon enough.

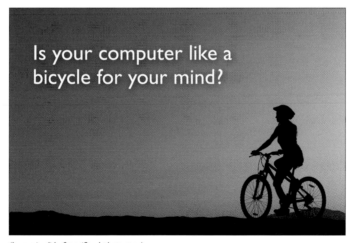

(Image in slide from iStockphoto.com.)

Paper, a Whiteboard, Post-it Notes, or a Stick in the Sand

My favorite tools for preparing a presentation (or any other project for that matter) usually consist of a large pad of yellow legal paper and colored pens, a moleskin storyboard book, or if I am in my office, a large whiteboard. As wonderful as digital technology is, I don't think anything is as quick, easy, and immediate as a simple pad and pencil, and nothing gives me space to jot down ideas quite like a massive whiteboard.

Most businesspeople and even college students do all the preparation of their presentations directly in slideware. In this regard, we can learn a lot from professional designers. Most professional designers—even young, new media designers who've grown up on computers—usually do much of their planning and brainstorming on paper.

This became very clear to me one day at Apple when I visited a senior director on one of the creative teams to get his input on a project. He said he had sketched out a lot of ideas to show me. I assumed that he had prepared some slides or a movie or at least printed out some color images in Illustrator or Photoshop to show me. But when I arrived at his office, I found that the beautiful Apple Cinema Display on his desk was off. (I learned later that this talented creative director worked for days without ever turning on his Mac.) Instead, he had sketched out his ideas on a scroll of white paper that stretched about five meters across his office wall. This large scroll was a combination of hand-drawn images and text resembling a large comic strip. The creative director started at one end of the "strip" and walked me through his ideas, stopping occasionally to add a word or graphic element. After our meeting, he rolled up his sketches and said "take 'em with you." Later, I would incorporate his ideas into our internal presentation using a computer.

*"If you have the ideas,
you can do a lot without machinery.
Once you have those ideas,
the machinery starts working for you....
Most ideas you can do pretty darn well
with a stick in the sand."*

—*Alan Kay*
(*Interview in* Electronic Learning, *April 1994*)

Pen and Paper

I spend a lot of time working outside my office in coffee shops, in parks, and while riding on the Japanese Bullet Train (*Shinkansen*) on my trips to Tokyo. And although I have a MacBook Air or iPad with me at virtually all times, it is pen and paper that I use to privately brainstorm, explore ideas, make lists, and generally sketch out my ideas. I could use the computer, but I find—as many do—that the act of holding a pen in my hand to sketch out ideas seems to have a greater, more natural connection to my right brain and allows for a more spontaneous flow and rhythm for visualizing and recording ideas. Compared to sitting at a keyboard, the act of using paper and pen to explore ideas, and the visualization of those ideas, seems far more powerful. It's certainly simple.

Whiteboards

I often use a large whiteboard in my office to sketch out my ideas. The whiteboard works for me because I feel uninhibited and free to brainstorm and sketch ideas on a bigger scale. I can also step back (literally) and imagine how it might flow logically when slides are added later. The advantage of a whiteboard (or chalkboard) is that you can use it with small groups to record concepts and directions. As I write down key points and assemble an outline and structure, I can draw quick ideas for visuals, such as charts or photos that will later appear in the slides. I draw sample images that I can use to support a particular point, say, a pie chart here, a photo there, perhaps a line graph in this section, and so on.

You may be thinking that this is a waste of time: Why not just go into software and create your images there so you do not have to do it twice? Well, the fact is, if I tried to create a storyboard first on the computer, it would actually take longer, as I would constantly have to go from normal view to slide sorter view to see the whole picture. The analog approach (paper or whiteboard) to sketching out my ideas and creating a rough storyboard really helps solidify and simplify my message in my own head. I then have a far easier time laying out those ideas in PowerPoint, Keynote, Prezi, and so on. I usually do not even have to look at the whiteboard or legal pad when I am on the computer because the analog process itself gave me a clear visual image of how I want the content to flow. I glance at my notes for reminders about the visuals I thought of using at certain points and then go to iStockphoto.com or to my own library of high-quality stock images to find the perfect image.

Post-it Notes

Large sheets of paper and marking pens—as "old school" as they may seem—can be wonderful, simple tools for initially sketching out your ideas and recording the ideas of others. When I was at Apple, I sometimes led brainstorming sessions by sticking large Post-its on the wall. I wrote ideas down or others stepped up to the front and sketched out their ideas "the old-fashioned way" while arguing their point or elaborating on others' ideas. It was messy, but it was a good mess. By the end of the session, the walls were filled with large Post-its, which I then took back to my office and stuck on my own walls. As we developed the structure and visuals for the presentation, we often referred to the sheets on the walls, which were on display for days or weeks. Having the content on the walls made it easier to see the big picture. It also made it easier to see what items could be cut and which were clearly essential to the core message.

Although you may be using digital technology to create your visuals and display them when you deliver your presentation, the act of speaking and connecting to an audience—to persuade, sell, or inform—is very much analog. For this reason, it only seems natural to go analog while preparing and clarifying your presentation's content, purpose, and goals.

Slowing Down to See

Slowing down is not just good advice for a healthier, happier, more fulfilling life, but it is also a practice that leads to greater clarity. Your instinct may be to say this is ridiculous—business is all about speed. First to innovate. First to market. First and fast.

What I am talking about here, however, is a state of mind. You have many things on your plate, no doubt. You are busy. But "busy" is not really the problem. Sure, there never seems to be enough time in the day to do things the way you would prefer to do them, and we all face time constraints. But time constraints can also be a great motivator, bringing a sense of urgency that stimulates creative thinking and the discovery of solutions to problems. The problem today, though, is not "busy" but "busyness."

Busyness is that uncomfortable feeling you have of being rushed, distracted, and a bit unfocused and preoccupied. Although you may be accomplishing tasks, you wish you could do better. You know you can. But in spite of your best intentions, you find it difficult to create a state of mind that is contemplative rather than reactionary. You try. You take a deep breath. You begin to think about the big presentation next week. So you launch your application and begin to think. Then the office phone rings, but you let it go to voicemail because your boss is calling you on your mobile phone at the same time. "Need TPS reports ASAP!" she says. Then your e-mail notifies you that you've got new messages, including one from your biggest client with the subject line "Urgent! TPS reports missing!!!" Then your coworker pops his head in the door, "Hey, did you hear about the missing TPS reports?" So you get to work reacting even though you know that dealing with the reports could actually wait until another time. In this sort of environment, it is nearly impossible to slow down.

Busyness kills creativity. Busyness leads to the creation and display of a lot of cluttered presentation visuals that substitute for engaging, informative, and provocative meetings, seminars, or keynote speeches where actual conversations could and should be taking place. But people feel rushed, even frantic. So they slap together some slides from past presentations and head off to their presentation. Communication suffers...the audience suffers. Yes, we're all insanely busy, but this is just all the more reason we owe it to ourselves and our audiences not to waste time with perfunctory "slideshows from hell." To do something better takes a different mindset, and it takes time and space away from "busyness."

When you think about it, the really great creatives—designers, musicians, even entrepreneurs, programmers, etc.—are the ones who see things differently and who have unique insights, perspectives, and questions. (Answers are important, but first come questions.) For many of us, this special insight and knowledge, as well as plain ol' gut feeling and intuition, can only come about when slowing down, stopping, and seeing all sides of our particular issue. It does not matter if you are a scientist, engineer, medical doctor, or businessperson. When you prepare a presentation, you are a "creative," and you need time away from the computer and dealing with digital outlines and slides. And whenever possible, you also need time alone.

One reason many presentations are so ineffective is that people today just do not take—or do not have—enough time to step back and really assess what is important and what is not. They often fail to bring anything unique, creative, or new to the presentation. This is not because they are not smart or creative beings, but because they did not have the time alone to slow down and contemplate the problem. Seeing the big picture and finding your core message may take some time alone "off the grid." There are many ways to find solitude, and you don't even have to be alone. I find a very pleasant form of solitude, for example, at a Starbucks in central Osaka, where the friendly staff know me by name. It's a bustling café but also cozy and relaxing with loads of overstuffed sofas and chairs and jazz playing softly in the background. And I am left alone.

I'm not suggesting that more time alone is a panacea for a lack of ideas or that it necessarily leads to more creativity or better solutions. But I think you will be pleasantly surprised if you can create more time every day, week, month, and year to experience solitude. For me, solitude helps achieve greater focus and clarity while also allowing me to see the big picture. Clarity and the big picture are the fundamental elements missing from most presentations.

I don't want to overly romanticize solitude. Too much "alone time" obviously can be a bad thing as well, yet in today's busy world, too much solitude is a problem faced by few of us. For most professionals, finding some time alone can be a great struggle indeed.

The Need for Solitude

Many believe solitude is a basic human need, and to deny it is unhealthy for both mind and body. Dr. Ester Buchholz, a psychoanalyst and clinical psychologist who passed away in 2004 at the age of 71, did quite a bit of research on solitude during her career—she called it "alone time." Dr. Buchholz thought society undervalued solitude and alone time and overvalued attachment. Dr. Buchholz thought periods of solitude were important if we were to tap our creative potential. "Life's creative solutions require alone time," she said. "Solitude is required for the unconscious to process and unravel problems." The second half of Dr. Buchholz's quote appears in the slide below, a slide I have used in some of my talks on creativity.

"Others inspire us, information feeds us, practice improves our performance, but we need quiet time to figure things out, to emerge with new discoveries, to unearth original answers."

— Ester Buchholz

Image in slide from iStockphoto.com.

We cannot see our reflection
in running water.

It is only in still water
that we can see.

—Taoist proverb

(Image in slides on these two pages from iStockphoto.com.)

In order to be open to creativity, one must have the capacity for constructive use of solitude. One must overcome the fear of being alone.

—Rollo May

Asking the Right Questions

It is said that Buddha described the human condition as much like that of a man who has been shot with an arrow. The situation is both painful and urgent. But let's imagine that instead of asking for immediate medical assistance for his predicament, the man asks for details about the bow that shot the arrow. He asks about the manufacturer of the arrow. He wonders about the background of the people who made the bow and arrow, how they arrived at the color choice, what kind of string they used, and so on. The man asks many inconsequential questions, overlooking the immediate problem.

Our lives are a bit like this. We often do not see the reality right in front of us because we chase ephemeral things such as larger salaries, the perfect job, a bigger house, more status, etc., and we worry about losing what we have. The Buddhist would say life is filled with *dukkha* (suffering, pain, loss, a feeling of dissatisfaction)—we need only to open our eyes to see this. In a similar way, the current state of business and academic presentation brings about a fair amount of "suffering" in the form of ineffectiveness, wasted time, and general dissatisfaction, both for the presenter and the audience.

There is much discussion today among professionals on the issue of how to make presentations and presenters better. For them, the situation is both "painful and urgent" in a sense. It's important. Yet much of the discussion focuses on software applications and techniques. What application should I get? Should I get a Mac or a PC? What animations and transitions are best? What is the best remote control? This is not completely inconsequential, but it often dominates discussions on presentation effectiveness. The focus on technique and software often distracts us from what we should be examining. Many of us spend too much time fidgeting with and worrying about bullets and images on slides during the preparation stage instead of thinking about how to craft the story that is the most effective, memorable, and appropriate for our audience.

The Wrong Questions

In obsessing on technique and tricks and effects, we are a bit like the man who has an arrow stuck in him: Our situation is urgent and painful, yet we are asking the wrong questions and focusing on that which is relatively inconsequential.

Two of the more inconsequential questions I get—and I get these a lot—are "How many bullets should I use per slide?" and "How many slides per presentation is good?" My answer? "It depends on a great many things… how about zero?" This gets people's attention, but it's not the most popular answer. I'll deal with the bullet points question in the chapter on slide design (Chapter 6). As for how many slides are best, that really is the wrong question. There are too many variables involved to make a concrete rule. I have seen long, dull presentations from presenters who used only five slides and content-rich, engaging presentations from presenters who used more than 200 slides (and vice versa). The number of slides is not the point. If your presentation is successful, the audience will have no idea how many slides you used, nor will they care.

Questions We Should Be Asking

OK, so you're alone. You've got a pad and a pen. You're relaxed, and your mind is still. Now imagine that presentation you get to give (notice I did not say "have to give") next month...or next week or (gulp!) tomorrow. Jot down the answers to these questions:

- How much time do I have?
- What's the venue like?
- What time of the day will I be speaking?
- Who is the audience?
- What is their background?
- What do they expect of me?
- Why was I asked to speak?
- What do I want them to do?
- What visual medium is most appropriate for this particular situation and audience?
- What is the fundamental purpose of my talk?
- What's the story here?
- And this is the most fundamental question of all, stripped down to its essence:

What is my core point?

Or put it this way: If the audience will remember only one thing (and you'll be lucky if they do), what do you want it to be?

Two Questions: What Is Your Point? Why Does It Matter?

A lot of the presentations I attend feature a person from a specialized field giving a talk—usually with the help of multimedia—to an audience of business people who are not specialists in the presenter's technical field. This is a common presentation situation. For example, an expert in the area of biofuel technology may be invited to give a presentation to a local chamber of commerce about the topic and about what his company does. Recently, I attended such an event, and after the hour-long talk was over, I realized the presentation was a miracle of sorts: until that day I didn't think it was possible to listen to someone make a presentation with slides in my native language of English and still not understand a single point that was made. Not one. *Nada*. I wanted my hour back.

The wasted hour was not the fault of the software or bad slides, however. The presentation would have been greatly improved if the presenter had simply kept two questions in mind while preparing for the talk: What is my point? And why does it matter?

It's hard enough for presenters to find their core message and express it in a way that is unambiguously understood. But why does it matter? This is where people really stumble. Often, the presenter is so close to his material that the question of why it should matter simply seems too obvious to make explicit. Yet that is what people (including most audiences) are hoping you'll tell them. "Why should we care?" That's going to take persuasion, emotion, and empathy in addition to logical argument. Empathy comes into play in the sense that the presenter must understand not everyone will see what to him is obvious, and others may understand well but not see why it should matter to them. When preparing material for a talk, good presenters try to put themselves in the shoes of their audience members.

To get back to my wasted hour, the presenter, who was smart, accomplished, and professional, failed before he even started. The slides looked as if they were the same ones used in previous presentations to more technical audiences, an indication that he had not thought first and foremost about his audience that day. He failed to answer the important question: "Why does it matter?" In the preparation stage, he also failed to remember that presentation opportunities such as this one are about leaving something important behind for the audience.

Dakara Nani? (So What?)

In Japanese, I often say to myself, "*Dakara nani*?" or "*Sore de...?*" which translates roughly as "So what?" or "Your point being...?" I say this often while I am preparing or helping others prepare their material.

When building the content of your presentation, you should always put yourself in the shoes of the audience and ask, "So what?" Really ask yourself the tough questions throughout the planning process. For example, is your point relevant? It may be cool, but is it important to further your story, or is it included only because it seems impressive to you? Surely you have been in an audience and wondered how the presenter's information was relevant or supported his core point. If you can't answer that question, then cut that bit of content out of your talk.

Can You Pass the Elevator Test?

If *Dakara nani* does not work for you, then check the clarity of your presentation's core message with the elevator test. This exercise forces you to "sell" your message in 30–45 seconds. Imagine this situation: You are scheduled to pitch a new idea to the head of product marketing at your company, one of the leading technology manufacturers in the world. Both schedules and budgets are tight; this is an extremely important opportunity if you succeed in getting the OK from the executive team. When you arrive at the admin desk outside the vice president's office, she comes out with her coat and briefcase in hand and says, "Sorry, something's come up. Give me your idea as we walk down to my car." Could you sell your idea in the elevator ride and the walk to the parking lot? Sure, the scenario is unlikely, but it's possible. What is more likely, however, is for you to be asked to shorten your talk down from, say, 20 minutes to 5 minutes or from a scheduled hour to 30 minutes on short notice. Could you do it? You may never have to, but practicing what you would do in such a case forces you to get your message down and make your overall content tighter and clearer.

(Image in slide from iStockphoto.com.)

(Image in slide from iStockphoto.com.)

Handouts Can Set You Free

If you create a proper handout for your presentation during the preparation phase, then you will not feel compelled to say everything about your topic in your talk. Preparing a proper document—with as much detail as you think necessary—frees you to focus on what is most important for your particular audience on your particular day. If you create a proper handout, you will also not worry about the exclusion of charts, figures, or related points. Many presenters include everything under the sun in their slides "just in case" or to show they are "serious people." It is common to create slides with lots of text and detailed charts, etc., because the slides will also serve as a leave-behind document. This is a big mistake (see the upcoming sidebar, "Create a Document, Not a Slideument"). Instead, prepare a detailed handout, and keep the slides simple. And never distribute a printed version of your slides as a handout. Why? David Rose, expert presenter and one of New York City's most successful technology entrepreneurs, puts it this way:

> *"Never, ever hand out copies of your slides, and certainly not before your presentation. That is the kiss of death. By definition, since slides are speaker support material, they are there in support of the speaker... YOU. As such, they should be completely incapable of standing by themselves, and are thus useless to give to your audience, where they will simply be guaranteed to be a distraction. The flip side of this is that if the slides can stand by themselves, why the heck are you up there in front of them?"*

> —*David S. Rose*

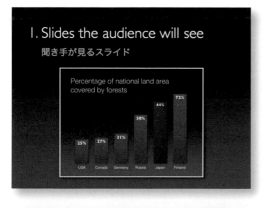

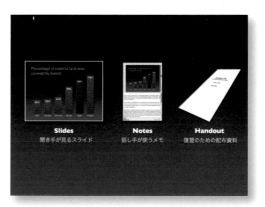

Three Parts of a Presentation

If you remember that there are three components to your presentation—the visuals, your notes, and the handout—then you will not feel the need to place so much information in your slides or other multimedia. Instead, you can place that information in your notes (for the purpose of rehearsing or as a backup) or in the handout. This point has been made by presentation experts such as Cliff Atkinson, yet most people still fill their slides with volumes of text and hard-to-see data and simply print out their slides instead of creating a separate leave-behind document.

(I have used the four slides on this page while making this point during my live talks on presentation design.)

Create a Document, Not a Slideument

Slides are slides. Documents are documents.
They aren't the same thing. Attempts
to merge them result in what I call the
"slideument." The creation of the slideument
stems from a desire to save time. People
think they are being efficient—a kind of
kill-two-birds-with-one-stone approach
or *iiseki ni cho* in Japanese. Unfortunately
(unless you're a bird), the only thing "killed"
is effective communication. Intentions are
good, but results are bad. This attempt
to save time reminds me of a more fitting
Japanese proverb: *Nito o oumono wa itto mo
ezu* or "Chase two hares and get none."

Projected slides should be as visual as possible and support your points quickly,
efficiently, and powerfully. The verbal content, the verbal proof, evidence, and
appeal/emotion come mostly from your spoken word. But your handouts are
completely different. With those, you aren't there to supply the verbal content
and answer questions, so you must write in a way that provides at least as much
depth and scope as your live presentation. Often, however, even more depth and
background information are appropriate because people can read much faster than
you can speak. Sometimes, a presentation is on material found in a speaker's book
or a long journal article. In that case, the handout can be quite concise; the book
or research paper is where people can go to learn more.

Do Conferences Encourage Slideumentation?

As proof that we live in a world dominated by bad presentations, many
conferences today require speakers to follow uniform slide guidelines and submit
their files far in advance. The conference then takes these "standardized slide
decks" and prints and places them in a large conference binder or includes them
on the conference DVD for attendees to take home. Conference organizers are
implying that a cryptic series of slides with bullet points and titles makes for both
good visual support in your live presentation and credible documentation of your
presentation content long after your talk has ended. This forces the speaker into
a catch-22 situation. The presenter must say to herself: "Do I design visuals that
clearly support my live talk, or do I create slides that more resemble a document
to be read later?" Most presenters compromise and shoot for the middle,

resulting in poor supporting visuals for the live talk and a series of document-like slides filled with text and other data that do not read well (and are therefore not read). A series of small boxes with text and images on sheets of paper do not a document make.

The slideument isn't effective, it isn't efficient, and it isn't pretty. Attempting to have slides serve both as projected visuals and as stand-alone handouts makes for bad visuals and bad documentation. Yet this is a typical approach. PowerPoint and other digital presentation tools are effective for displaying visual information that helps tell your story, make your case, prove your point, and engage your audience. Presentation software tools *are not* good, however, for making written documents. That's what word processors are for.

So why don't conference organizers request that speakers send a written document (with a specified maximum page length) that covers the main points of their presentation with appropriate detail and depth? A Word or PDF document written in a concise and readable fashion with a bibliography and links to even more details for those who are interested would be far more effective. When I get home from a conference, do organizers really think I'm going to attempt to read pages of printed slides? One does not read a printout of a two-month-old slide deck. Rather, one guesses, decodes, and attempts to glean meaning from the series of low-resolution titles, bullets, charts, and clip art—at least they do that for a while…until they give up. With a written document, however, there is no reason for shallowness or ambiguity (assuming one writes well).

To be different and effective, use a well-written, detailed document for your handout and well-designed, simple, intelligent graphics for your visuals. And while it may require more effort on your part, the quality of your visuals and takeaway documents will be dramatically improved.

Avoiding the Slideument

The slide below on the left displays obesity rates for 30 countries in two formats. The table and bar graph were made in Excel and pasted into slideware. It is common for people to take detailed data such as this from Excel or Word documents and paste them into display slides for a presentation. But it's rarely necessary to include all this data in an on screen visual for a short live talk. If it is necessary to examine so much data during the presentation, put the table and charts in a handout. (The low resolution and limited real estate of display screens makes it difficult to read labels at such small sizes anyway.) It is usually better to use only the data that truthfully and accurately support your point. In this example, the point is to show how the U.S. obesity rate is much higher than the rate in Japan. It is not necessary to show the rates for so many other countries; this information is better included in a handout.

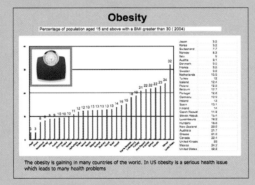

Instead of using a detailed chart that will appear cluttered and difficult to read, try creating a simpler visual for the slide and place the detailed charts and tables in a leave-behind document where you have more space to present the details in a proper layout.

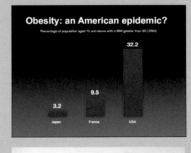

The Benefit of Planning Well

If you prepare well, and really get your story down pat—well enough to pass the elevator test—then you can sell your core message well in any situation. A friend of mine, Jim in Singapore, sent me an e-mail sharing a good example of what can happen when you do this work in the preparation stage.

> *Dear Garr... got this new prospect and have been trying to get in front of the guy for months. Finally get the word he'll see me next week. I know he is a super short attention span guy so I used a simple approach and agonized over the content and the key message and then the graphics. We get to the office and begin with the usual small talk that starts a meeting and suddenly I realize we've gone over the points of the presentation in our conversation and he has agreed to move forward. Then he looks at his watch and says great to see you thanks for coming in. As we walk out of the building the two guys that work for me say hey you never even pulled out the presentation and he still bought the deal—that was great!*
>
> *Meanwhile I'm in a complete funk: "What about all my preparation time? He never even saw my presentation. What a waste of time putting the whole thing together!" Then the light went on. Presentation preparation is about organizing thoughts and focusing the storytelling so it's all clear to your audience. I was able to articulate the points because I had worked those through in the preparation of the presentation. Even the graphics had made me think the presentation through and became a part of the presentation even though the audience never saw them.*

Jim makes an excellent point here. If you prepare well, the process *itself* should help you really know your story. With proper preparation, you should be able to still tell your story even if the projector breaks or if the client says, "To heck with the slides, just give it to me straight."

The planning stage should be the time when your mind is most clear with all barriers removed. I love technology, and I think slideware can be very effective in many situations. But for planning, go analog: Use a paper and pen, whiteboards, a notepad in your pocket as you walk down the beach with your dog...whatever works for you. Peter Drucker said it best: "The computer is a moron." You and your ideas (and your audience) are all that matter. So try getting away from the computer in the early stages when your creativity is needed most. For me, clarity of thinking and the generation of ideas come when my computer and I are far apart.

The purpose behind getting off the grid, slowing down, and using paper or whiteboards during the preparation stage is to better identify, clarify, and crystallize your core message. Again, if your audience remembers only one thing, what should that be? And why? By getting your ideas down and your key message absolutely clear in your mind and on paper first, you'll be able to organize and design slides and other multimedia that support and magnify your content.

In Sum

• Slow down your busy mind to see your problem and goals more clearly.

• Find time alone to see the big picture.

• For greater focus, try turning off the computer and going analog.

• Use paper and pens or a whiteboard to record and sketch out your ideas.

• Key questions: What's your main (core) point? Why does it matter?

• If your audience remembers only one thing, what should it be?

• Preparing a detailed handout keeps you from feeling compelled to cram everything into your visuals.

Crafting the Story

During your time off the grid, you brainstormed alone or perhaps with a small group of people. You stepped back to get the big picture, and you identified your core message. You now have a clearer picture of the presentation content and focus even if you do not have all the details worked out yet. The next step is to give your core message and supporting messages a logical structure. Structure will help bring order to your presentation and make it easier for you to deliver it smoothly and for your audience to understand your message easily.

Before you go from analog to digital—taking your ideas from sketches on paper and laying them out in PowerPoint or Keynote—it is important to keep in mind what makes your ideas resonate with people. What makes some presentations absolutely brilliant and others forgettable? If your goal is to create a presentation that is memorable, then you need to consider how you can craft messages that stick.

One of the components for creating sticking messages is story. We tell stories all the time. Think about times you may have been camping with a group of people, taking a tiny step back to a more primitive time, where the evening develops into long sessions of storytelling around the campfire. There is something very natural, compelling, and memorable about both telling and listening to stories.

What Makes Messages Stick?

Most of the great books that will help you make better presentations are not specifically about presentations at all, and they are certainly not about how to use slideware. One such book is *Made to Stick* (Random House) by Chip and Dan Heath. The Heath brothers were interested in what makes some ideas effective and memorable and others utterly forgettable. Some stick, and others fade away. Why? What the authors found—and explain simply and brilliantly in their book—is that "sticky" ideas have six key principles in common: simplicity, unexpectedness, concreteness, credibility, emotions, and stories. And yes, these six compress nicely into the acronym SUCCESs.

The six principles are relatively easy to incorporate into messages—including presentations and keynote addresses—but most people fail to use them. Why? The authors say the biggest reason most people fail to craft effective or "sticky" messages is because of what they call the "Curse of Knowledge." The Curse of Knowledge is essentially the condition whereby the deliverer of the message cannot imagine what it's like not to possess his level of background knowledge on the topic. When he speaks in abstractions to the audience, it makes perfect sense to him but him alone. In his mind, it seems simple and obvious. The six principles—SUCCESs—are your weapons, then, to fight your own Curse of Knowledge (we all have it).

Here's an example the authors used early in their book to explain the difference between a good, sticky message and a weak garden-variety message. Look at these two messages, which address the same idea. One of them should seem very familiar to you.

> *"Our mission is to become the international leader in the space industry through maximum team-centered innovation and strategically targeted aerospace initiatives."*

Or

> *"...put a man on the moon and return him safely by the end of the decade."*

The first message sounds similar to CEO-speak today and is barely comprehensible, let alone memorable. The second message—which is actually from a 1961 speech by John F. Kennedy—has every element of SUCCESs, and it motivated a nation toward a specific goal that changed the world. JFK, or at least his speechwriters, knew that abstractions are not memorable, nor do they motivate. Yet how many speeches by CEOs and other leaders contain phrases such as "maximize shareholder value yada, yada, yada?" Here's a quick summary of the six principles from *Made to Stick* that you should keep in mind when crystallizing your ideas and crafting your message for speeches, presentations, or any other form of communication.

- **Simplicity.** If everything is important, then nothing is important. If everything is a priority, then nothing is a priority. You must be ruthless in your efforts to simplify—not dumb down—your message to its absolute core. We're not talking about stupid sound bites here. Every idea can be reduced to its essential meaning if you work hard enough. For your presentation, what's the key point? What's the core? Why does (or should) it matter?

- **Unexpectedness.** You can get people's interest by violating their expectations. Surprise people. Surprise will get their interest. But to sustain their interest, you have to stimulate their curiosity. The best way to do that is to pose questions or open holes in people's knowledge and then fill those holes. Make the audience aware that they have a gap in their knowledge and then fill that gap with the answers to the puzzle (or guide them to the answers). Take people on a journey.

- **Concreteness.** Use natural speech and give real examples with real things, not abstractions. Speak of concrete images, not of vague notions. Proverbs are good, say the Heath brothers, at reducing abstract concepts to concrete, simple, but powerful (and memorable) language. For example, the expression *iiseki ni cho* or "kill two birds with one stone" is easier than saying something like "let's work toward maximizing our productivity by increasing efficiency across many departments." And the phrase "go to the moon and back" by JFK (and Ralph Kramden before him)? Now that's concrete. You can visualize that.

- **Credibility.** If you are famous in your field, you may have built-in credibility (but even that does not go as far as it used to). Most of us, however, do not have that kind of credibility, so we reach for numbers and cold, hard data to support our claims as market leaders and so on. Statistics, say the Heath brothers, are not inherently helpful. What's important is the context and the meaning. Put it in terms people can visualize. "Five hours of battery life" or "Enough battery life to watch your favorite TV shows nonstop on your iPod during your next flight from San Francisco to New York"? There are many ways to establish credibility—a quote from a client or the press may help, for example. But a long-winded account of your company's history will just bore your audience.

- **Emotions.** People are emotional beings. It is not enough to take people through a laundry list of talking points and information on your slides; you must make them *feel* something. There are a million ways to help people feel something about your content. Images are one way to have audiences not only understand your point better but also have a more visceral and emotional connection to your idea. Explaining the devastation of the Katrina hurricane and floods in the United States, for example, could be done with bullet points, data, and talking points. But images of the aftermath and the pictures of the human suffering that occurred tell the story in ways words, text, and data alone never could. Just the words "Hurricane Katrina" conjure vivid images in your mind. Humans make emotional connections with people, not abstractions.

When possible, put your ideas in human terms. "100 grams of fat" may seem concrete to you, but for others it is an abstraction. A picture of an enormous plate of greasy French fries, two cheeseburgers, and a large chocolate shake will hit people at a more visceral level. "So that's what 100 grams of fat looks like!"

100 grams of fat

• **Stories.** We tell stories all day long. It's how humans have always communicated. We tell stories with our words and even with our art and music. We express ourselves through the stories we share. We teach, we learn, and we grow through stories. In Japan, it is a custom for a senior worker (*sempai*) to mentor a younger worker (*kohai*) on various issues concerning company history and culture and how to do the job. The *sempai* does much of his informal teaching through storytelling although nobody calls it that. Once a younger worker hears the story of what happened to the poor guy who didn't wear his hardhat on the factory floor, he never forgets the lesson (and he never forgets to wear his hardhat). Stories get our attention and are easier to remember than lists of rules. People love Hollywood, Bollywood, and indie films. People are attracted to "story." Why is it, though, that when the majority of smart, talented, story-loving people have the chance to present, they usually resort to generating streams of vaguely connected information rather than stories or examples and illustrations? Great ideas and presentations have an element of story to them.

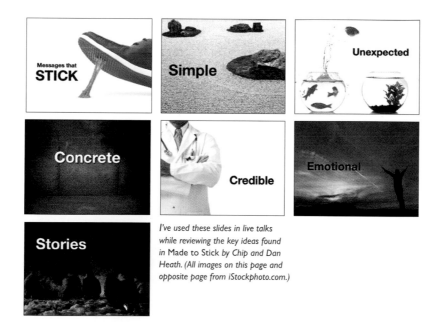

I've used these slides in live talks while reviewing the key ideas found in Made to Stick *by Chip and Dan Heath. (All images on this page and opposite page from iStockphoto.com.)*

I believe this nation should commit itself to achieving the goal, before this decade is out, of landing a man on the Moon and returning him safely to the Earth.

— John F. Kennedy
May 25, 1961

Story and Storytelling

Before there was the written word, humans used stories to transfer culture from one generation to the next. Stories are who we are, and we are our stories. Stories may contain analogies or metaphors, powerful tools for bringing people in and helping them understand our thoughts clearly and concretely. The best presenters illustrate their points with stories, often personal ones. The easiest way to explain complicated ideas is through examples or by sharing a story that underscores the point. If you want your audience to remember your content, then find a way to make it more relevant and memorable by strengthening your core message with good, short, stories or examples.

Good stories have interesting, clear beginnings; provocative, engaging content in the middle; and a clear conclusion. I am not talking about fiction here. I am talking about reality, regardless of the topic. Remember that documentary films, for example, "tell the story" of whatever it is they are reporting on. Documentaries do not simply tell facts; rather, they engage us with the story of war, scientific discovery, a dramatic sea rescue, climate change, and so on. We are wired to forget what our brains perceive as unimportant to our survival. Our conscious mind tells us to read the physical chemistry book over and over because we need to pass the class, but our brain keeps telling us this is dull, uninteresting, and unimportant to our survival. The brain cares about story.

The Power of Story

Story is an important way to engage the audience and appeal to people's need for logic and structure in addition to emotion. Humans are predisposed to remembering experiences in the narrative form; we learn best with a narrative structure. Humans have been sharing information aurally and visually far longer than we have been getting information by reading lists. A 2003 *Harvard Business Review* article on the power of story says storytelling is the key to leadership and communication in business: "Forget PowerPoint and statistics, to involve people at the deepest level you need to tell stories."

In an interview with the *Harvard Business Review*, legendary screenwriting coach Robert McKee suggests a big part of a leader's job is to motivate people to reach certain goals. "To do that she must engage their emotions," McKee says, "and the key to their hearts is story." The most common way to persuade people, says McKee, is with conventional rhetoric and an intellectual process that, in the business world, often consists of a typical PowerPoint presentation in which leaders build their case with statistics and data. But people are not moved by statistics alone, nor do they always trust your data. "Statistics are used to tell lies...while accounting reports are often BS in a ball gown." McKee says rhetoric is problematic because while we are making our case others are arguing with us in their heads using their own statistics and sources. Even if you do persuade through argument, says McKee, this is not good enough because "people are not inspired to act on reason alone." The key, then, is to aim to unite an idea with an emotion, which is best done through story. "In a story, you not only weave a lot of information into the telling but you also arouse your listener's emotion and energy," he says.

Look for the Conflict

A good story is not the beginning-to-end tale of how results meet expectations, McKee says. This is boring. Instead, it's better to illustrate the "struggle between expectation and reality in all its nastiness." What makes life interesting is "the dark side" and the struggle to overcome the negatives—struggling against negative powers is what forces us to live more deeply, says McKee. Overcoming negative powers is interesting, engaging, and memorable. Stories such as this are more convincing.

The biggest element a story has, then, is conflict. Conflict is dramatic. At its core, story is about a conflict between our expectations and cold reality. Story is about an imbalance and opposing forces or a problem that must be worked out. A good storyteller describes what it's like to deal with these opposing forces such as the difficulty of working with scarce resources, making difficult decisions, or undertaking a long journey of scientific discovery, and so on. People prefer to present only the rosy (and boring) picture. "But as a storyteller, you want to position the problems in the foreground and then show how you've overcome them," says McKee. If you tell the story of how you struggled with antagonists, the audience is engaged with you and your material.

Contrasts Are Compelling

Whether we are talking about graphic design or the components of a story, the principle of contrast is one of the most fundamental and important elements to include. Contrast is about differences, and we are hardwired to notice differences. You can see the principle of contrast everywhere in good storytelling, including filmmaking. For example, in *Star Wars IV*, there is obviously compelling contrast between the good and noble Rebel Alliance and the dark side of the Death Star and the evil empire. Yet great contrasts exist even between main characters in the story who are on the same side. The young, naïve, idealistic Luke Skywalker character contrasts with the old, wise, and realistic Obi-Wan Kenobi. The level-headed, diplomatic, young Princess Leia contrasts with the slightly cocky, irreverant, older Han Solo. These characters are compelling to millions of fans because of their inherent contrasts and the series of negotiations they go through as they deal with their differences. Even R2D2 and C3PO are engaging characters, in large part because of their strikingly different personalities. In your own presentations, look for contrasts such as before/after, past/future, now/then, problem/solution, strife/peace, growth/decline, pessimism/optimism, and so on. Highlighting contrasts is a natural way to bring the audience into your story and make your message more memorable.

Using Storytelling Principles in Presentations

You do not always have a lot of time to prepare your presentation or perhaps it is difficult to see what the story is, so here are three simple steps you can use to prepare virtually any presentation relatively quickly.

Basic elements to include in your story:

1. *Identify the problem.* (This could be a problem, for example, that your product solves.)
2. *Identify causes of the problem.* (Give actual examples of the conflict surrounding the problem.)
3. *Show how and why you solved the problem.* (This is where you provide resolution to the conflict.)

Essentially, that's it: Introduce the problem you have (or did have) and how you will solve it (or did solve it). Give examples that are meaningful and relevant to your audience. Remember, story is sequential: "This happened, and then this happened, and therefore this happened, and so on." Take people on a journey that introduces conflict and then resolves that conflict. If you can do this, you will be miles ahead of most presenters who simply recall talking points and broadcast lists of information. Audiences tend to forget lists and bullet points, but stories come naturally to us; it's how we've always attempted to understand and remember the bits and pieces of experience. Robert McKee's point is that you should not fight your natural inclination to frame experiences into a story; instead, embrace this and tell the story of your experience of the topic to your audience.

Stories and Emotions

Our brains tend to recall experiences or stories that have a strong emotional element to them. The emotional components of stories are what helps them be remembered. Earlier this year, four students in my Japanese labor management class did a presentation on employment security in Japan. Three days later, when I asked other students to recall the most salient points of the presentation, what they remembered most vividly were not the labor laws, the principles, and the changes in the labor market in Japan but, rather, the topic of *karoshi*, or suicide related to work, and the issue of suicides in Japan, topics that were quite minor points in the hour-long presentation. Perhaps five minutes out of the hour were spent on the issue of karoshi, but that's what the audience remembered most. It's easy to understand why. The issue of death from overworking and the relatively high number of suicides are extremely emotional topics that are not often discussed. The presenters cited actual cases and told stories of people who died as a result of karoshi. The stories and the connections they made with the audience caused these relatively small points to be remembered because emotions such as surprise, sympathy, and empathy were all triggered.

Kamishibai: Lessons in Visual Storytelling from Japan

Kamishibai is a form of visual and participatory storytelling that combines the use of hand-drawn visuals with the engaging narration of a live presenter. *Kami* (紙) means "paper" and *shibai* (芝居) means "play/drama." The origins of kamishibai can be traced back to various picture storytelling traditions in Japan, which include *etoki* and *emaki* scrolls and other forms of visual storytelling dating back centuries. However, the form of kamishibai that one thinks of today developed around 1929 and was popular in the 1930s, and '40s, all but dying out with the introduction of television later in the 1950s. Typical kamishibai consisted of a presenter who stood to the right of a small wooden box or stage that held the 12–20 cards featuring the visuals that accompanied each story. This miniature stage was attached to the storyteller's bicycle, from which he sold candy to the small children who gathered before the show (this was originally how the storyteller could make a little money). The presenter changed the cards by hand, varying the speed of the transition to match the flow of the story he was telling. The best kamishibai presenters did not read the story, but instead kept their eyes on the audience and occasionally on the current card in the frame.

Kamishibai is as different from picture books as modern presentation visuals are different from documents. In the case of a picture book, there can be more visual details and text. However, picture books are usually read alone unlike kamishibai which is designed to be presented in front of a larger group gathered around the presenter and his visuals.

Although kamishibai is a form of visual storytelling that became popular more than eighty years ago, the lessons from this craft can be applied to modern multimedia presentations. Tara McGowan, who wrote *The Kamishibai Classroom* (Libraries Unlimited), says that kamishibai visuals are more like the frames in a movie. "Kamishibai pictures are designed to be seen only for a few [moments], so extraneous details detract from the story and open up the possibilities of misinterpretation." It's important to design each card, she says, "...to focus the audience's attention on characters and scenery that are most important at any given moment. If clarity and economy of expression are the goals, it would be hard to find a more perfect medium." It's easy to imagine how we can apply the same spirit of kamishibai to our modern-day presentations that include the use of multimedia and a screen. Here are five tips from kamishibai that we can apply to our presentations today:

1. Visuals should be big, bold, clear, and easy to see.
2. Allow graphic elements to fill the frame and bleed off the edges.
3. Use visuals in an active way, not a decorative one.
4. Aim to carefully trim back the details.
5. Make your presentation—visuals and narration—participatory.

Stories and Authenticity

I have seen pretty good (though not great) presentations with average delivery and graphics that were relatively effective because the speaker told relevant stories in a clear, concise manner to support his points in a voice that was human, not formal. Rambling streams of consciousness will not get it done; audiences need to hear (and see) your points illustrated in real language.

Earlier this year, in fact, I saw a fantastic presentation by the CEO of one of the most famous foreign companies in Japan. The CEO's PowerPoint slides were of mediocre design, and he made the mistake of having not one but two assistants off to the side to advance his slides to match his talk. The assistants seemed to have difficulty with the slideware, and often the wrong slide appeared behind the presenter, but this powerful man simply shrugged his shoulders and said "...ah, doesn't matter. My point is..." He moved forward and captivated the audience with his stories of the firm's past failures and recent successes, stories that contained more captivating and memorable practical business lessons than most business students will get in an entire semester or more.

It is true that the presentation would have been even better if the slides had been better designed and used properly, but in this particular case, the CEO gave a powerful and memorable presentation in spite of those shortcomings. Trust me, this is very rare in the world of CEO presentations. There are four essential reasons for his success that night: (1) He knew his material inside and out, and he knew what he wanted to say. (2) He stood front and center and spoke in a real, down-to-earth language that was conversational yet passionate. (3) He did not let technical glitches get in his way. When they occurred, he moved forward without missing a beat, never losing his engagement with the audience. (4) He used real, sometimes humorous, anecdotes to illustrate his points, and all his stories were supremely poignant and relevant, supporting his core message.

What made this CEO's presentation so compelling and memorable was that it was, above all, authentic. His stories were from his heart and from his gut, not from a memorized script. We do not tell a story from memory alone; we do not need to memorize a story that has meaning to us. If it is real, then it is in us. Based on our research, knowledge, and experience, we can tell it from our gut. Internalize your story, but do not memorize it line by line. You can't fake it. You believe in your story, or you do not. And if you do not, no amount of hyped-up, superficial enthusiasm or conviction will ever make your time with an audience meaningful. If you do not believe it, do not know it to be true, how can you connect and convince others with your words in story form? Your words will be hollow.

It's Not Just About Information

People who possess loads of information in a particular field have historically been in hot demand and able to charge high fees for access to their stuffed, fact-filled brains. This was so because facts used to be difficult to access. Not anymore. In an era when information about seemingly anything is only a mouse click away, just possessing information is hardly the differentiator it used to be. What is more important today than ever before is the ability to synthesize the facts and give them context and perspective. Picasso once said, "Computers are useless for they can only give answers." Computers and Google can indeed give us routine information and facts we need. What we want from people who stand before us and give a talk is that which data and information alone cannot: meaning.

Remember we are living in a time when fundamental human talents are in great demand. Anyone—indeed any machine—can read a list of features or give a stream of facts to an audience. That's not what we need or want. What we yearn for is to listen to an intelligent and evocative—perhaps, at times, even provocative—human being who teaches, inspires, or stimulates us with knowledge and meaning, context, and emotion in a way that is memorable.

And this is where story comes in. Information plus emotion and visualization wrapped in unforgettable anecdotes are the stuff that stories are made of. If presentations were only about following a linear, step-by-step formula for distributing information and facts, then no one would be complaining about boring presentations today; after all, the majority of presentations still follow just such a formula. And if designing visuals for your presentation were simply a matter of following a list of rules, then why on earth should we keep wasting our time creating slides and other multimedia? Why not simply outsource our facts, outlines, and bullet points to someone who could do it more cheaply?

But presentations are not just about following a formula for transferring facts in your head to the heads of those sitting before you by reciting a list of points on a screen. (If it were, why not send an e-mail and cancel the presentation?) What people want is something fundamentally more human. They want to hear the story of your facts.

Finding Your Voice

The voice of the storyteller is also important. We pay attention to well-spoken narratives that sound human, that are spoken in a conversational voice. Why do we pay more attention to conversational speech from a storyteller or presenter? It may be because our brain—not our conscious mind—does not know the difference between listening to (or reading) a conversational narrative and actually being in a conversation with a person. When you are in a conversation with someone, you are naturally more engaged because you have an obligation to participate. Formal speech and writing devoid of any emotion is extremely difficult to stay with for more than a few minutes. Your conscious mind has to remind you to "stay awake, this is important!" But someone who speaks in a natural, conversational style is far easier to stay engaged with.

Majora Carter speaks with a "human voice" at the TED Conference in 2005, explaining her fight for environmental justice in the South Bronx. (Photo: TED/ leslieimage.com)

Dana Atchley (1941–2000)
A Digital Storytelling Pioneer

Dana Atchley was a legend and pioneer in the field of digital storytelling. His clients included Coke, EDS, Adobe, Silicon Graphics, and many others. He even worked with Apple as a charter member of the AppleMasters program. In the '90s. Atchley was helping senior executives create emotional, compelling talks that used the latest technology to create "digital stories" that connected with and appealed to audiences in a more visceral, visual, emotional, and memorable way. If Atchley had not passed away at age 59 in 2000, presentations—even in the world of business— might be far more appropriate, engaging, and effective today. Here's what Dana Atchley said about digital storytelling:

> *"Digital storytelling combines the best of two worlds: the 'new world' of digitized video, photography, and art, and the 'old world' of telling stories. This means the 'old world' of PowerPoint slides filled with bullet point statements will be replaced by a 'new world' of examples via stories, accompanied by evocative images and sounds."*

Here's what Dan Pink, writing for *Fast Company*, said about Dana Atchley and his mission in this excerpt from a 1999 article titled "What's Your Story?"

> *"[W]hy does communication about business remain so tedious? Most businesspeople describe their dreams and strategies—their stories—just as they've been doing it for decades: stiffly, from behind a podium, and maybe with a few slides. Call it 'Corporate Sominex.' Digital storytelling is more than a technique. In fact, it's become something of a movement among both artists and businesspeople."*

This bit from the *Fast Company* article makes the future of business presentations sound so promising. I get excited reading this and thinking about the possibilities. Yet, since 1999, how much has really changed? Some people today are indeed using digital technology in presentations the way Atchley envisioned. But there is such a long, long way to go before we rid the business world of the "corporate Sominex" phenomenon.

Learn more about Dana Winslow Atchley III and his brilliant contributions on the Next Exit website: *www.nextexit.com.*

The Process

The problem with slideware applications—PowerPoint, in particular, because it's been around longer and influenced a generation—is that they have, by default, guided users toward presenting in outline form with subject titles and bullet points grouped under each topic heading. This is similar to the good ol' topic sentence in a high school composition class. It seems logical enough, but it is a structure that makes the delivery of the content utterly forgettable for the audience. Storyboarding can help. If you take the time in this part of the preparation stage to set up your ideas in a logical fashion in storyboard format, you can then visualize the sequential movement of your content narrative and the overall flow and feel of the presentation.

Because you have already identified your core message away from the computer, you can now begin to create a storyboard that will give shape to the story of your short presentation. Storyboards have their origins in the movie industry but are used often in business, particularly in the field of marketing and advertising.

One of the simplest and most useful features of PowerPoint and Keynote is the Slide Sorter view (Light Table view in Keynote). You can take your notes and sketches and create a storyboard directly in PowerPoint or Keynote, or you can remain "analog" a bit longer and draft a storyboard on paper or by using Post-its or a whiteboard, etc.

Each situation and each individual is different, and there are indeed many paths to better presentations, including better preparation. My personal approach moving from rough analog sketches to digital slides is not uncommon at all. I have been surprised, however, that for the most part, individual professionals, entrepreneurs, and students usually just open up slideware, type about a dozen subject slides, and then fill them with talking points. This is not an effective approach, nor is it a method I recommend although it is common.

Below is the five-step approach I usually take. I sometimes skip the third and fourth steps, but I find it works well when a group is planning the presentation. For students working on a group presentation, step 3 is vital.

Step 1

Brainstorming. Step back, go analog, get away from the computer, tap into the right brain, and brainstorm ideas. You need not show restraint here. Editing comes later. In brainstorming, quantity matters. Here, I put ideas down on cards or sticky notes and place them on a table or whiteboard. This is something you can do by yourself or in a group. When working in a group, do not judge others' ideas. Simply write them down and place them with the others for the time being. At this stage, even crazy ideas are OK because the offbeat ideas may lead to more practical yet still compelling supporting ideas later on. As the great Linus Pauling once said, "The best way to have a good idea is to have a lot of ideas."

Brainstorming "off the grid" away from the computer. This is very much a nonlinear process, and the more ideas the better. Here ideas are suggested and quickly jotted down on Post-it notes.

Step 2

Grouping and identifying the core. In this step, I look to identify one key idea that is central (and memorable) from the point of view of the audience. What is the "it" that I want them to get? I use "chunking" to group similar ideas while looking for a unifying theme. The presentation may be organized into three parts, so first I look for the central theme that will be the thread running through the presentation. There is no rule that says your presentation should have three sections or three "acts." However, three is a good number to aim for because it is a manageable constraint and generally provides a memorable structure. Regardless of how many sections I use, there is only one theme. It all comes back to supporting that key message. The supporting structure—the three parts—is there to back up the core message and the story.

Participants in a Presentation Zen seminar at the Kyoto Institute of Technology in Japan begin to group and identify core messages after their brainstorming session.

Step 3

Storyboarding off the computer. I take the Post-it notes roughly arranged in step 2 and lay them out in a sequence. The advantage of this method (compared to the Slide Sorter view in PowerPoint or the Light Table view in Keynote) is that I can easily add content by writing on an additional Post-it and sticking it under the appropriate section without ever losing sight of the structure and flow. In software, I have to switch to Slide mode to type or add an image directly on a slide and then go back to the Slide Sorter mode to see the big-picture structure. Alternatively—and this is very popular with my Japanese business students—you can print out blank slides, 12 slides per sheet, which essentially gives you a larger version of a Moleskine Storyboard. If you want larger slides, you can print out nine slides or six. You then can tape these to the wall or spread them out on the desk, keeping them in a notebook when you're done. As shown below, you can sketch your visuals and write down your key points in a printed version of slideware notes.

After eliminating many ideas created in their brainstorming session, these participants in Japan begin to build the structure of their presentation by arranging their messages in sequence. This part is still a bit messy as they are continuing to eliminate and add new ideas to improve their overall story.

Step 4

Sketch your visuals. Now that you have identified a clear theme, a core takeaway message, and two or three sections containing an appropriate amount of detail (including data, stories, quotes, facts, and so on), you can begin to think about visuals. How can you visualize your ideas to make them more memorable and accessible to your audience? Using a sketchbook and sticky notes, or even scratch paper, begin to change the words on your paper or sticky notes into rough sketches of images—images that eventually will become high-quality photography, quantitative displays, charts, slides featuring quotations, etc. You can use some of the same sticky notes to sketch the rough visualizations you used in step 3, and you can replace some of those notes with new sticky notes.

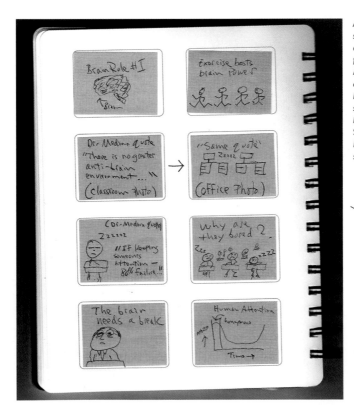

A sample of just eight slides from a section of a presentation on audience engagement, citing some of the ideas from the book Brain Rules *by John Medina. I am not going to win an art competition for my quick sketches, but that does not matter. These rough sketches are just for me. (Image shown here is of the* Presentation Zen Storyboarding Sketchbook *(New Riders). Later, I used them to assemble simple visuals on the computer (opposite*

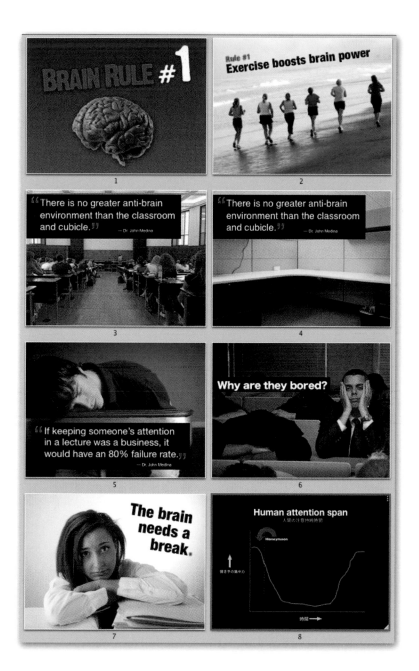

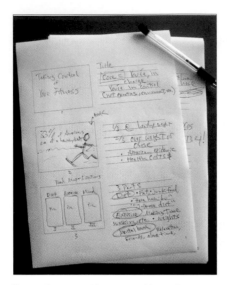

Shown here are the title slide, the "hook," and the roadmap of the talk. The actual "hook" and background section of the obesity problem covered several slides before I introduced the roadmap/outline. (Images used in these slides from iStockphoto.com.)

You can also use your ideas generated in step 3 to create rough sketches in printed blank slides from your slideware. In this example, key points of the narration behind each visual are written on the side. These sketches became the slides on the right.

Step 5

Storyboarding on the computer. If you have a clear sense of your structure, you can skip steps 3 and 4 and start building the flow of your presentation directly in slideware (though I recommend going through those storyboarding and sketching steps if the stakes of the presentation are high). Create a blank slide using a template of your choosing (or the simplest version of your company's template if you must use it). I usually choose a blank slide and then place a simple text box inside it with the size and font I'll use most often. (You can create multiple master slides in PowerPoint and Keynote.) Then I duplicate several of these slides because they will contain the visual content of my presentation: short sentences or single words, images, quotes, charts and graphs, etc. The section slides—what presentation guru Jerry Weismann calls *bumper slides*—should be a different color with enough contrast that they stand out when you see them in the Slide Sorter view. You can have these slides hidden, so you see them only when planning in Slide Sorter view if you prefer; however, in my case, these slides will serve to give visual closure to one section and open the next section.

Now that I have a simple structure in the Slide Sorter view, I can add visuals that support my narrative. I have an introduction in which I introduce the issue or "the pain" and introduce the core message. I then use the next three sections to support my assertions or "solve the pain" in a way that is interesting and informative but that never loses sight of the simple core message.

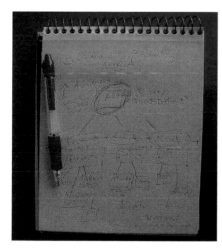

ABOVE *Rough outline from step 2 for a presentation I created on presentation delivery called "The Naked Presenter." Here, I used a simple pad instead of Post-it notes. However, from the ideas on this pad, I sketched rough visuals and put down key words on Post-it notes to build the structure just as in step 4 (not shown here).*

RIGHT *The start of the storyboarding process in step 5 for the same presentation. Although the sketches from step 4 are not shown here, from the outline structure from step 2, you can see the simple structure before slides were added to the appropriate sections. The total number of slides ended up being more than 200.*

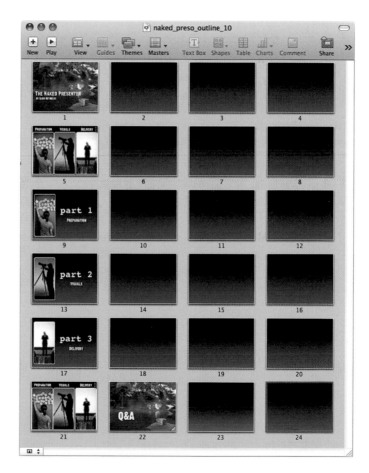

Nancy Duarte

CEO of Duarte, Inc., the world's leading presentation and story firm. Clients include the greatest brands and thought leaders in the world.
www.duarte.com

Nancy Duarte talks about storyboards and the process of presentation design.

Much of our communication today exhibits the quality of intangibility. Services, software, causes, thought leadership, change management, company vision—they're often more conceptual than concrete, more ephemeral than firm. And there's nothing wrong with that. But we regularly struggle when communicating these types of ideas because they are essentially invisible. It's difficult to share one's vision when there's nothing to see. Expressing these invisible ideas visually, so they feel tangible and actionable, is a bit of an art form, and the best place to start is not with the computer. A pencil and a sheet of paper will do nicely.

Why take this seemingly Luddite approach? Because presentation software was never intended to be a brainstorming or drawing tool. The applications are simply containers for ideas and assets, not the means to generate them. Too many of us have fallen into the trap of launching our presentation application to prepare our content. In reality, the best creative process requires stepping away from technology and relying on the same tools of expression we grew up with—pens and pencils. Quickly sketch lots of ideas. These can be words, diagrams, or scenes; they can be literal or metaphorical. The only requirement is that they express your underlying thoughts. The best thing about this process is that you don't need to figure out how to use drawing tools or where to save the file. Everything you need you already have (and don't say you can't

draw; you're just out of practice). This means you can generate a large quantity of ideas in a relatively short amount of time.

For me, one idea per sticky note is preferable. And I use a Sharpie. The reason? If it takes more space than a Post-it and requires more detail than a Sharpie can provide, the idea is too complex. Simplicity is the essence of clear communication. Additionally, sticky notes make it easy to arrange and rearrange content until the structure and flow feels right. On the other hand, many people on my team use a more traditional storyboarding approach, preferring to linearly articulate detailed ideas. That's fine, too. The point is not to prescribe exactly how to work but to encourage you to generate a lot of ideas.

Often ideas come immediately. That's good, but avoid the potential pitfall of going with the first thing that comes to mind. Continue to sketch and force yourself to think through several more ideas. It takes discipline and tenacity—especially when it feels like you solved it on the first try. Explore words and word associations to generate several ideas. Use mind-mapping and word-storming techniques to create yet more ideas (digital natives might prefer mind-mapping software for this phase). Stronger solutions frequently appear after four or five ideas have percolated to the top. Continue generating ideas even if they seem to wander down unrelated paths; you never know what you might find, after all. Then, once you've generated an enormous amount of ideas, identify a handful that meet the objective of the vision or concept you're trying to communicate. It matters less what form they take at this point than that they get your message across.

By the way, cheesy metaphors are a cop-out. If you feel tempted to use a picture of two hands shaking in front of a globe, put the pencil down, step away from the desk, and think about taking a vacation or investigating aromatherapy. Push yourself to generate out-of-the-box ideas. Take the time and spend the creative energy because the payoff will be a presentation people not only remember, but one they take action on.

Now, begin to sketch pictures from the ideas. These sketches become visual triggers that spark more ideas. The sketching process should be loose and quick—doodles really. Generate as many pictures as you can. In this way, sketching serves as proof-of-concept because ideas that are too

complex, time consuming, or costly will present themselves as ripe for elimination. Don't worry about throwing things away—that's why you generated a lot of ideas in the first place. In fact, you're ultimately going to have to throw all of them away except for one (designers recognize this as the destructive aspect of the creative process; it's a good thing). Some of the ideas you generate may require multiple scenes built across a few slides versus a snapshot on a single slide. On the other hand, sometimes it's as simple as using the perfect picture or diagram. Focus on whatever works best, not on the idea that's easiest to execute.

Be prepared to enlist the help of a designer. (You did plan far enough ahead to make sure you've got one available, right?) There's no shame in seeking professional help; what's important is effective communication, regardless of whether or not you have the skill set to execute it.

Brainstorming with Nancy Duarte (bottom right) and two of her staff, Ryan and Michaela, at Duarte headquarters in Silicon Valley.

Moxie Software

www.moxiesoftware.com

Many times the best concept doesn't exist as a ready-to-go stock photo. Some ideas are so unique, you have to create them from scratch—creating a memorable visual.

Duarte, Inc. created multiple concepts for Moxie Software. The client picked Concept 2 shown on the opposite page. All of Duarte's planning and ideating was done by hand so that they would not be restricted by cliché concepts.

Design: Duarte, Inc.

Concept 1 *The Illustrations and scenes were made out of yarn. Each slide connects to the next which gives an illusion of panning through a scene when transitioning to the next frame.*

Concept 2 *This concept required photography to be taken in-house at Duarte, Inc. and many of the images were custom-designed to create the desk and office scenes as an environment.*

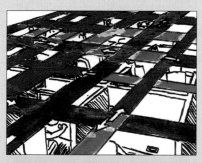

If you feel tempted to use a picture of two hands shaking in front of a globe, put the pencil down, step away from the desk, and think about taking a vacation or investigating aromatherapy.

—Nancy Duarte

Editing and Restraint

I am a bit of a *Star Wars* geek. Over the years, as I've learned more about the incredible creativity (and hard work) behind Lucas's films, I realized we mere mortals can learn much about presentations (which are essentially opportunities to tell our story) by listening to the advice of master storytellers such as George Lucas.

As I researched the numerous interviews over the years of Lucas talking about the making of the *Star Wars* films, one key idea often discussed was the importance of editing like mad to get the story down to about two hours. To do this, they scrutinized every scene to make sure that it actually contributed to the story—no matter how cool it was. If, during the editing process, a scene was judged to be superfluous to the story in any way, it was cut (or trimmed if the length was the only problem). They were very keen on keeping to the two-hour format because this was in the best interest of the audience.

We have all seen scenes from movies that left us scratching our heads wondering how they contributed to the story. Perhaps the director felt the scene was so technically cool or difficult to make that he just couldn't stand the thought of not including it in the film. But that would be a poor reason to include a scene. As far as presentations go, we have all seen people include data, facts, graphics, or a seemingly unrelated anecdote that just did not contribute to the speaker's overall point (which we were probably at a loss to find anyway). Presenters often include superfluous items because they are proud of their work and want to show it off even when it does not help support the speaker's particular point.

Moral of the story: Always keep the audience in mind by first keeping your talk as short as you can and still doing an effective job telling your story. Second, after you have prepared your presentation, go back and edit like crazy, eliminating parts that are not absolutely crucial to your overall point or purpose. You must be ruthless. When in doubt, cut it out.

It's paramount that we be ruthless editors of our own material. We have to make tough choices, choosing even not to do something (because it is not meeting your standards, for example). The hardest thing can be deciding to cut and even abandon material altogether, but it must be done.

Many people are not good at editing their presentations because they are afraid. They figure nobody ever got fired for including too much information. Better safe than sorry, they say. But this leads to lots of material and wasted time. Covering your butt by including everything under the sun is not the right place to be coming from; it's not the most appropriate motivation. It is, after all, only a presentation, and no matter how much you include, someone will say, "Hey, why didn't you say _____!" Difficult people are out there, but don't play to them, and do not let fear guide your decisions.

Designing a tight presentation that has the facts right but does so by giving simple, concrete anecdotes that touch people's emotions is not easy work, but it's worth it. Every successful presentation has elements of story to it. Your job is to identify the elements of your content that can be organized in a way that tells a memorable story.

In Sum

- Make your ideas sticky by keeping things simple, using examples and stories, looking for the unexpected, and tapping into people's emotions.

- A presentation is never *just* about the facts.

- Brainstorm your topic away from the computer, chunk (group) the most important bits. Identify the underlying theme, and be true to that theme (core message) throughout the creation of the presentation.

- Make a storyboard of your ideas on paper—and then use software to lay out a solid structure that you can see.

- Show restraint at all times, and bring everything back to the core message.

design

Our lives are frittered away by detail; simplify, simplify.

— Henry David Thoreau

5

Simplicity:
Why It Matters

As our daily lives have become more complex, more and more people look to incorporate simplicity into their lives. But finding simplicity in the workplace seems harder these days. Professionally, people are terrified of being simple for fear of being labeled a lightweight. So "when in doubt, add more" is often the guiding principle.

There is a fundamental misunderstanding of simplicity and what it means to be simple today. Many people confuse simple, for example, with simplistic, simplism, or that which is dumbed down to the point of being deceptive or misleading. To some people, simple means a kind of oversimplification of an issue, which ignores complexities and creates obfuscation and outright falsehoods. Politicians are often guilty of this type of oversimplification. But this is not the kind of simplicity I am talking about. The kind of simplicity I mean does not come from a place of laziness or ignorance; rather, it comes from an intelligent desire for clarity that gets to the essence of an issue, which is not easy to do.

Simplicity—along with other precepts such as restraint and naturalness—are key ideas found in Zen and the Zen arts: arts such as the tea ceremony, *haiku*, *ikebana*, and *sumi-e*, which can take many years or, indeed, a lifetime to master. There is nothing easy about them, although when performed by a master, they may seem beautifully simple. It is difficult to give a definition of simplicity, but when I say we need to create messages and design visuals that are simple, I am not talking about taking shortcuts, ignoring complexities, or endorsing meaningless sound bites and shallow content. When I use the word *simple* (or *simplicity*), I am referring to the term as essentially synonymous with clarity, directness, subtlety, essentialness, and minimalism. Designers, such as interaction designers, are constantly looking for the simplest solution to complex problems. The simple solutions are not necessarily easiest for them, but the results may end up being the "easiest" for the end user.

The best visuals are often ones designed with an eye toward simplicity. Yet this says nothing about the specifics of a visual presentation. That will depend on the content and context. For example, even the best visuals used in support of a presentation for one audience on, say, quantum mechanics may appear complicated and confusing to a different audience. Simplicity is often used as a means to greater clarity. However, simplicity can also be viewed as a consequence of our careful efforts to craft a story and create supporting visuals that focus on our audience's needs in a clear and meaningful way.

Simplicity is an important design principle, but simplicity itself is not a panacea. Though people usually err on the side of making presentation slides more complicated than they need to be, it is indeed possible to be "too simple." Simplicity is the goal, but as Albert Einstein said, "Everything should be made as simple as possible, but not simpler."

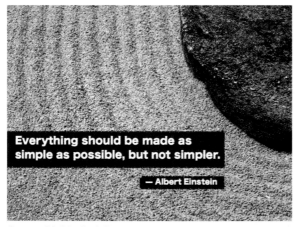

(Image in slide from iStockphoto.com.)

Steve Jobs and the Zen Aesthetic

Steve Jobs was one of the best presenters the world of business has ever seen. When Jobs spoke on stage, he was clear and to the point. While he was CEO of Apple, his presentations generated a lot of positive buzz and released a wave of viral communication about the presentation's content. This happened in part because the content was easily grasped and remembered by both the media and regular customers. You can't "spread the word" if you don't get what the word is. With Jobs's public presentations, there was both verbal and visual clarity.

Jobs was a student of Zen and was influenced early on by the Japanese aesthetic. "I have always found Buddhism, especially Japanese Zen Buddhism in particular, to be aesthetically sublime," Jobs told biographer Walter Isaacson, author of the book *Steve Jobs*. "The most sublime thing I've ever seen are the gardens around Kyoto. I'm deeply moved by what that culture has produced, and it's directly from Zen Buddhism." Jobs's personal style and approach to presentations certainly embodied an essence of simplicity and clarity that was remarkable and rare among CEOs or leaders of any kind.

Part of his great clarity could be seen in the visuals that accompanied his talks. There was a kind of "Zen aesthetic" to his presentation visuals. In Jobs's slides, you could see evidence of restraint, simplicity, and a powerful yet subtle use of empty space. Clutter and the nonessential were strictly forbidden.

Bill Gates, one of the most powerful and philanthropic businessmen of our time, always provided a lesson in contrast to Jobs's visual simplicity—although Gates has gotten much better in the last couple of years, and his presentation visuals for his TED talks and Gates Foundation presentations have been good.

However, the typical style of presentation that Gates became known for over the years was very similar to the style of slide presentation we still see too much of today—presentations with the kind of slides that hurt more than help with audience engagement. Problems with the visuals included too many elements on one slide, overuse of bullet points (including long lines of text), cheesy-looking images, too many colors, overused gradation techniques, weak visual communication priority, and an overall impression of clutter on screen.

Both Jobs and Gates used slides to complement their talks over the years. The biggest difference was that Jobs's visuals were a big part of his talk. The visuals were a necessary component of the talk, not just ornamentation or notes to remind him what to say. Jobs used the slides to help him tell a story, and he interacted with them in a dynamic yet natural way, rarely turning his

back on the audience. Jobs used the huge backlit screen
behind him in the same spirit that a filmmaker uses the
screen: to help tell a story. A filmmaker uses actors, visuals,
and effects to convey his message. Jobs used visuals and
his own words and natural presence to tell his story. Jobs's
slides always flowed smoothly with his talk.

In Bill Gates's case, however, the slides were often not
only of low aesthetic quality, they simply did not really
help his narrative. Gates's slides were often not really
necessary; they were more of an ornament or a decoration
off to the side. In many instances, Gates would have been
better off just pulling up a stool and sharing his ideas and
then answering questions that audience members could
have submitted before the talk so he could select those
he would answer. You don't have to use slideware for every
presentation, but if you do, the visuals should seem a part
of the show, not something "over there" off to the side.

I have always admired Bill Gates for his work with
education and the great work his foundation does today.
But when it came to his public keynote presentations back
in his Microsoft days—and the visuals that accompanied
those talks—there was much he could have learned
about "presenting differently" from Steve Jobs. Gates's
keynotes were not terrible; they were just very average and
unremarkable. His PowerPoint-driven style was normal and
typical, and his presentations were largely unmemorable as
a result. Bill Gates is a remarkable man; his presentations
should be remarkable too. Happily, he does seem to think
differently about his presentation visuals today, and his
presentations are better as a result.

The moral of the story for the rest of us is this: If you
are going to get up in front of a lot of people and say
the design of your strategy matters or the design of your
integrated software matters, then at the very least the
visuals you use—right here and right now, at this moment,
with this particular audience—also need to be the result of
thoughtful design, not hurried decoration.

Kanso, Shizen, Shibumi

Zen itself is not concerned with judging this design to be good or that design to be bad. Still, we can look to some of the concepts in the Zen aesthetic to help us improve our own visuals with an eye toward simplicity.

Kanso (Simplicity)

A key tenet of the Zen aesthetic is *kanso* or simplicity. In the *kanso* concept, beauty and visual elegance are achieved by elimination and omission. Says artist, designer, and architect Dr. Koichi Kawana, "Simplicity means the achievement of maximum effect with minimum means." When you examine your visuals, then, can you say that you are getting the maximum impact with a minimum of graphic elements, for example? When you take a look at Jobs's slides and Gates's slides of the past, how do they compare for *kanso*?

Shizen (Naturalness)

The aesthetic concept of naturalness or *shizen* "prohibits the use of elaborate designs and over refinement," according to Dr. Kawana. Restraint is a beautiful thing. Talented jazz musicians, for example, know never to overplay but instead to be forever mindful of the other musicians and find their own space within the music and the moment they are sharing. Graphic designers show restraint by including only what is necessary to communicate the particular message for the particular audience. Restraint is hard. Complication and elaboration are easy...and common. The suggestive mode of expression is a key Zen aesthetic. Dr. Kawana, commenting on the design of traditional Japanese gardens, says, "The designer must adhere to the concept of *miegakure* since Japanese believe that in expressing the whole, the interest of the viewer is lost."

Shibumi (Elegance)

Shibumi is a principle that can be applied to many aspects of life. Concerning visual communication and graphic design, *shibumi* represents elegant simplicity and articulate brevity, an understated elegance. In *Wabi-Sabi Style* (Gibbs Smith Publishers), authors James and Sandra Crowley comment on the Japanese deep appreciation of beauty in this sense:

"Their (Japanese) conceptualization relegates elaborate ornamentation and vivid color usage to the bottom of the taste levels...excess requires no real thought or creativity. The highest level of taste moves beyond the usage of brilliant colors and heavy ornamentation to a simple and subdued refinement that is the beauty of *shibumi*, which represents the ultimate in good taste through conscious reserve. This is the original 'less is more' concept. Less color—subdued and elegant usage of color, less clutter."

In the world of slide presentations, you do not always need to visually spell everything out. You do not need to pound every detail into the head of each member of your audience either visually or verbally. Instead, the combination of your words, along with the visual images you project, should motivate the viewer and arouse his imagination, helping him to empathize with your idea and visualize it beyond what is visible in the ephemeral PowerPoint slide before him. The Zen aesthetic values include (but are not limited to) the following:

- Simplicity
- Subtlety
- Elegance
- Suggestive rather than descriptive or obvious
- Naturalness (i.e., nothing artificial or forced)
- Empty space (or negative space)
- Stillness, tranquility
- Eliminating the nonessential

All of these principles can be applied to slide design, Web design, and so on.

Wabi-Sabi Simplicity

I first learned of *wabi-sabi* while studying *sado* (Japanese tea ceremony) many years ago in the Shimokita Hanto of Aomori, a rural part of northern Japan—a perfect place to experience traditional Japanese values and concepts. While studying *sado*, I began to appreciate the aesthetic simplicity of the ritual, an art that is an expression of fundamental Zen principles such as purity, tranquility, a respect for nature, and the desire to live in harmony with it.

The ideals of *wabi-sabi* come from Japan, and the origins are based on keen observations of nature. *Wabi* means "poverty" or lacking material wealth and all its possessions yet, at the same time, feeling free from dependence on worldly things, including social status. There is an inward feeling of something higher. *Sabi* means "loneliness" or "solitude," the feeling you might have while walking alone on a deserted beach deep in contemplation. These two concepts come together to give us an appreciation for the grace and beauty of a scene or a work of art while remaining fully aware of its ephemerality and impermanence.

Some Westerners may be familiar with the term *wabi-sabi* through *wabi-sabi*-inspired design, a kind of earthy interior design that is balanced, organic, free from clutter and chaos, and somehow quite beautiful in its simple presentation, never appearing ostentatious or decorated.

The ideals of *wabi-sabi* are most applicable to disciplines such as architecture, interior design, and the fine arts. But we can apply the principles to the art of digital storytelling (presentations with AV support or integration) as well. *Wabi-sabi* embraces the "less is more" idea that is often talked about—and often ignored—in today's society. Visuals created with a sense of *wabi-sabi* are never accidental, arbitrary, cluttered, or busy. They may be beautiful, perhaps, but never superfluous or decorative. They will be harmonious and balanced, whether symmetrical or asymmetrical. The elimination of distraction and noise can certainly help begin to make visuals with greater clarity.

A Zen garden is also a lesson in simplicity: open space without ornamentation, a few rocks carefully selected and placed, raked gravel. Beautiful. Simple. The Zen garden is very different from many gardens in the West that are absolutely filled with beauty, so much beauty, in fact, that we miss much of it. Presentations are a bit like this. Sometimes, we're presented with so much visual and auditory stimulation in such a short time that we end up understanding very little and remembering even less. We witnessed a large quantity of stuff, but is it not the quality of the evidence and the experience that matters, rather than, say, merely the amount of data or the length of the experience?

Living in Japan all these years, I have had many chances to experience the Zen aesthetic, either while visiting a garden, practicing *zazen* (meditation) in a Kyoto temple, or even while having a traditional Japanese meal out with friends. I am convinced a visual approach that embraces the aesthetic concepts of simplicity and the removal of the nonessential can have practical applications in our professional lives and can lead ultimately to a more enlightened design. I do not suggest you judge a presentation visual the same way you do a work of art. But understanding the essence of Zen simplicity can have practical applications in your creative work, including the design of your presentation visuals.

The Ryoan Ji Zen Garden in Kyoto, Japan. A reminder to include only what is essential. (Photo: iStockphoto.com.)

The "Fish Story"

After I presented for a large tech company in Silicon Valley, I received this note below from Deepak, an engineer in the audience. This little story illustrates the idea of reducing the nonessential.

Dear Garr... When you talked about reducing the text on the slides, I was reminded of a story from my childhood in India. If I remember it right, it goes like this:

> *When Vijay opened his store, he put up a sign that said: "We Sell Fresh Fish Here." His father stopped by and said that the word "We" suggests an emphasis on the seller rather than the customer, and is really not needed. So the sign was changed to "Fresh Fish Sold Here."*
>
> *His brother came by and suggested that the word "here" could be done away with—it was superfluous. Vijay agreed and changed the sign to "Fresh Fish Sold."*
>
> *Next, his sister came along and said the sign should just say "Fresh Fish." Clearly, it is being sold; what else could you be doing?*
>
> *Later, his neighbor stopped by to congratulate him. Then he mentioned that all passers-by could easily tell that the fish was really fresh. Mentioning the word fresh actually made it sound defensive as though there was room for doubt about the freshness. Now the sign just read: "FISH."*
>
> *As Vijay was walking back to his shop after a break he noticed that one could identify the fish from its smell from very far, at a distance from which one could barely read the sign. He knew there was no need for the word "FISH."*

By stripping down an image to essential meaning, an artist can amplify that meaning...

—Scott McCloud

Amplification Through Simplification

The Japanese Zen arts teach us that it is possible to express great beauty and convey powerful messages through simplification. Zen may not verbalize "amplification through simplification," but you can see this idea everywhere in the Zen arts. There is a style of Japanese painting called the "one-corner" style, for example, which goes back some 800 years and is derived from the concepts of *wabi* and *sabi*. Paintings in this style are very simple and contain much empty space. You may have a painting depicting a large ocean scene and empty sky, for example. In the corner, there is a small, old fishing canoe, hardly visible. It's the smallness and placement of the canoe that give vastness to the ocean and evoke a feeling of calm and an empathy for the aloneness the fisherman faces. Such visuals have few elements yet can be profoundly evocative.

Learning from the Art of Comics

We can learn about simplicity as it relates to presentation visuals from unexpected places, including—and this may surprise you—the art of comics. And the best place to learn this is from Scott McCloud's *Understanding Comics: The Invisible Art* (Harper Paperbacks). In this popular book, McCloud repeatedly touches on the idea of "amplification through simplification." McCloud says cartooning is a form of amplification through simplification because the abstract images in comics are not so much the elimination of detail as they are an effort to focus on specific details.

A key feature of many comics is their visual simplicity. Yet as McCloud reminds us, while casting an eye toward the wonderful world of Japanese comics, "simple style does not necessitate simple story." Many people (outside Japan at least) prejudge comics by their simple lines and forms as being necessarily simplistic and base, perhaps suitable for children and the lazy but not something that could possibly have depth and intelligence. Surely such a simple style found in comics cannot be illustrating a complex story, they say.

However, if you visit coffee shops around Tokyo University—Japan's most elite university—you will see stacks and stacks of comics (*manga*) on the shelves. There is nothing necessarily stupid about the genre of comics in Japan at all; in fact, you'll find brainiacs in all shapes and sizes reading comics here and, indeed, around the world.

The situation today is that most people have not been exposed to the idea of making a visual stronger by stripping it down to its essence. Less equals less in most people's eyes. If we apply this visual illiteracy to the world of presentations, you can imagine the frustration a young, enlightened professional must feel when her boss looks over her presentation visuals the day before her big presentation and says, "No good. Too simple. You haven't said anything with these slides! Where are your bullet points!? Where's the company logo!? You're wasting space—put some data in there!" She tries to explain that the slides are not the presentation but that she is the presentation and that the points will be coming from her mouth. She tries to explain that the slides contain a delicate balance of text and images and data designed to play a supportive yet powerful role in helping amplify her message. She attempts to remind her boss that they also have strong, detailed documentation for the client and that slides and documents are not the same. But her boss will have none of it. The boss is not happy until the PowerPoint deck looks like normal PowerPoints, you know, the kind used by serious people.

TO AMPLIFY, TRY TO SIMPLIFY!

We must do what we can to be firm, however, and remain open to the idea of amplification through simplification as much as possible. I am not suggesting you become an artist or that you should draw your own images. Rather, I am suggesting that you can learn a lot about how to present images and words together by exploring the so-called "low art" of comics. In fact, although presentation visuals were surely the farthest thing from McCloud's mind when he wrote the book, we can learn far more about effective communication for the conceptual age from it than we can from many books on PowerPoint. For example, early in the book, McCloud builds a definition of comics and finally arrives with this, a definition he admits is not written in stone:

> *"Juxtaposed pictorial and other images in deliberate sequence intended to convey information and/or to produce an aesthetic response in the viewer."*

It is easy to imagine, with some tweaking, how this could be applied to other storytelling media and presentation contexts as well. We do not have a good definition for "live presentation with slides," but a great presentation may indeed contain slides that are comprised of "juxtaposed pictorial and other images." And great presentations certainly have elements of sequence designed to "convey information and/or to produce an aesthetic response."

At the end of the book, McCloud gives us some simple, Zen-like wisdom. He's talking about writers, artists, and the art of comics, but this is good advice to live by no matter where our creative talents may lie. "All that's needed," he says, "...is the desire to be heard. The will to learn. And the ability to see."

When you get right down to it, it always comes back to desire, a willingness to learn, and the ability to really see. Many of us have the desire; it's the learning and seeing that's the hard part. McCloud says that in order for us to understand comics, we need to "clear our minds of all preconceived notions about comics. Only by starting from scratch can we discover the full range of possibilities comics offer." The same can be said for presentation design. Only by approaching presentations and presentation design with a completely open mind can we see the options before us. It is just a matter of seeing.

Redux: Simplicity Is Not Easy

Usually, we think about time in terms of "How can I save it?" Time is a constraint for us, but what if, when planning a presentation, we took the notion of saving time and looked at it from the point of view of our audience instead of our own personal desire to do things more quickly? What if it wasn't just about *our time,* but it was about *their time*? When I am in the audience, I appreciate it very much when I am in the presence of a speaker who is engaged, has done his homework, has prepared compelling visuals which add rather than bore, and generally makes me happy I have attended. What I hate more than anything—and I know you do too—is the feeling I get when I realize I am at the beginning of a wasted hour ahead of me.

Often, the approach I advocate may use more time, not less time, for you to prepare, but the time you are saving for your audience can be huge. Again, is it always about saving time for ourselves? Isn't it important to save time for others? When I save time for myself, I am pleased. But when I save time for my audience—by *not* wasting their time and instead by sharing something important with them—I feel inspired, energized, and rewarded.

I can save time on the front end, but I may waste more time for others on the back end. For example, if I give a completely worthless, one-hour, death-by-PowerPoint presentation to an audience of 200, that equals 200 hours of wasted time. But if I put in the time, say, 25 to 30 hours or more of planning and designing the message and the media, then I can give the world 200 hours of a worthwhile, memorable experience.

Software companies advertise time-saving features, which may help us believe we have saved time to complete a task such as preparing a presentation and simplified our workday. But if time is not saved for the audience—if the audience wastes its time because we didn't prepare well, design the visuals well, or perform well—then what does it matter that we saved one hour in preparing our slides? Doing things in less time sometimes does indeed feel simpler, but if it results in wasted time and wasted opportunities later, it is hardly simple.

In Sum

- Simplicity is powerful and leads to greater clarity, yet it is neither simple nor easy to achieve.

- Simplicity can be obtained through the careful reduction of the nonessential.

- As you design slides, keep the following concepts in mind: subtlety, grace, and understated elegance.

- Good designs have plenty of empty space. Think "subtract" not "add."

- While simplicity is the goal, it is possible to be too simple. Your job is to find the balance most appropriate to your situation.

6

Presentation Design: Principles and Techniques

When I was an employee with Sumitomo in the mid-1990s, I learned that Japanese businesspeople often use the term "case by case" (*keisu bai keisu*) when discussing details of future events or strategy. This frustrated me because I was accustomed to concrete plans, absolutes, and quick decision making. I learned, however, that context, circumstance, and a kind of "particularism" were very important to the Japanese with whom I worked.

Today, I might use Japanese expressions such as *jyoukyou ni yotte* (judgment depends on circumstance) or *toki to baai ni yotte* (depends on time and circumstance) when discussing the techniques and designs to use for a particular presentation, for example. I used to think that "it depends" was a weak statement, a cop-out of sorts. Now I see that it is wise. Without a good knowledge of the place and circumstance, and the content and context of a presentation, it is difficult to say this is "appropriate" and that is "inappropriate," let alone to judge what is "good" or "bad." There are no cookie-cutter approaches to design. Graphic design is as much art as science.

Nonetheless, there are some general guidelines that most appropriate and strong slide designs share. A few basic and fundamental concepts and design principles, if properly understood, can indeed help the average person create presentation visuals that are far more effective. One could fill several volumes with design principles and techniques: you can read more on the topic in my book *Presentation Zen Design* (New Riders). In this chapter, I'll exercise restraint and elaborate on only a few principles plus showcase practical examples and a few techniques. First, let's look at what is meant by design.

Presentation Design

A common misunderstanding about design is that it is something that comes at the end—like the frosting and the "Happy Birthday!" on a cake. But this is not what I mean by design. For me, design does not wait until the end. Rather, it comes at the beginning, right from the start. Design is necessary to organize information in a way that makes things clearer; it can make things easier for the viewer or the user. Design is also a medium for persuasion. It is not decoration.

Design is about people creating solutions that help or improve the lives of other people—often in profound ways, and often in ways that are quite small and unnoticed. When we design, we need to be concerned with how other people interpret our design solutions and messages. Design is not art, although there is art in it. Artists can, more or less, follow their creative impulses and create whatever it is they want to express. But designers work in a business environment. At all times, designers need to be aware of the end user and how best to solve (or prevent) a problem from the user's point of view. Art is good or bad in and of itself. Good art may move people; it may change their lives in some way. If so, wonderful. But good design *must* necessarily have an impact on people's lives, no matter how seemingly small. Good design changes things.

Design is much more than aesthetics, yet things that are well-designed, including graphics, often have high aesthetic quality. Well-designed things look good. In the world of design, there is more than one solution to a single problem. You need to explore, but ultimately you need to look for the most appropriate solution for the problem, given the context of your information. Design is about making conscious decisions about inclusion and exclusion.

In the case of presentation visuals, graphics must be free of errors and they must be accurate. But our visuals—like it or not—also touch our audiences at an emotional level. People make instant judgments about whether something is attractive, trustworthy, professional, too slick, and so on. This is a visceral reaction—and it matters.

General Design Principles

In the following sections, I'll take you through seven interconnected design principles that are fundamental to good slide design. The first two—signal-to-noise ratio and picture superiority effect—are broad concepts with practical applications to slide design. The third—empty space—helps us look at slides in a different way and appreciate the power of what is not included to make visual messages stronger. The final four principles are grouped together in what I call "the big four" of basic design principles: contrast, repetition, alignment, and proximity. Designer and author Robin Williams first grouped and applied these four basic principles to the art of document design in her best-selling book *The Non-Designer's Design Book* (Peachpit Press). I'll show you how to apply the principles to improving slide design.

Signal-to-Noise Ratio

The signal-to-noise ratio (SNR) is a principle borrowed from more technical fields such as radio communications and electronic communication in general. The principle itself, however, applies to design and communication problems in virtually any field. For our purposes, the SNR is the ratio of relevant to irrelevant elements and information in a slide or other display. The goal is to have the highest signal-to-noise ratio possible in your slides. People have a hard time coping with too much information. There is simply a limit to a person's ability to process new information efficiently and effectively. Aiming for a higher SNR attempts to make things easier for people. Understanding can be hard enough without bombarding audience members with excessive and nonessential visuals that are supposed to be playing a supportive role.

Ensuring the highest possible signal-to-noise ratio means communicating (designing) clearly with as little degradation to the message as possible. You can degrade the visual message in many ways, including selecting inappropriate charts, using ambiguous labels and icons, and unnecessarily emphasizing items such as lines, shapes, symbols, and logos that do not play a key role in support of the message. In other words, if the item can be removed without compromising the visual message, then strongly consider minimizing or removing it. For example, lines in grids or tables can often be quite thin or light—or even removed. Footers, logos, and the like can usually be removed with positive results (assuming your company allows you to do this).

In *Visual Explanations: Images and Quantities, Evidence and Narrative* (Graphics Press), Edward Tufte refers to an important principle, called "the smallest effective difference," that is in harmony with SNR. "Make all visual distinctions as subtle as possible," says Tufte, "but still clear and effective." If the message can be designed with fewer elements, then there is no point in using more.

OPPOSITE PAGE *Compare the original slides on the left to those with an improved signal-to-noise ratio on the right. To achieve this, I removed nonessential elements and minimized other elements. Note that in the second example, I converted the pie chart to a bar chart, which makes the differences much easier to see.*

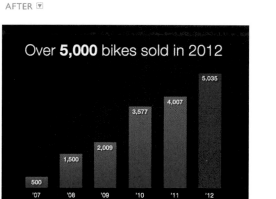

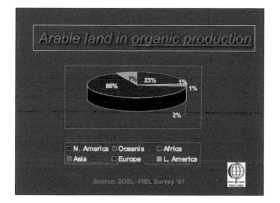

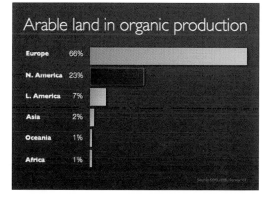

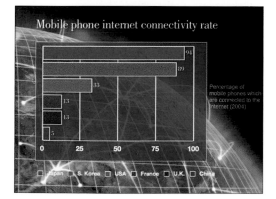

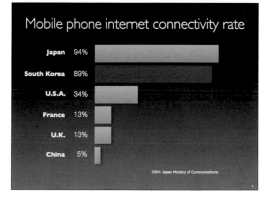

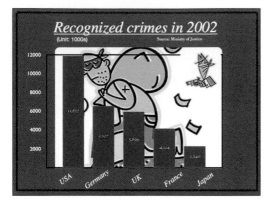

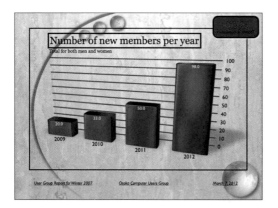

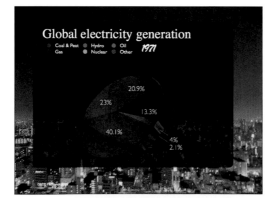

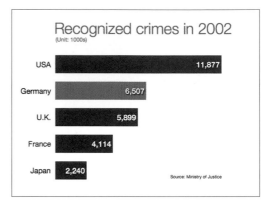

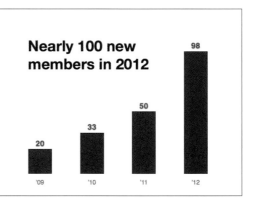

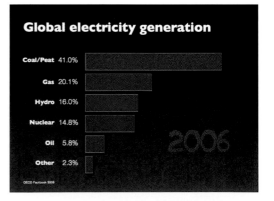

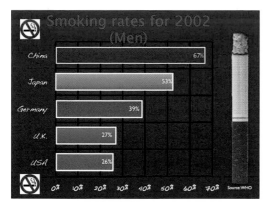

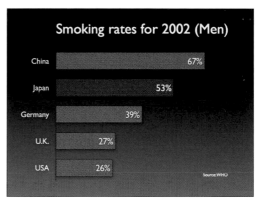

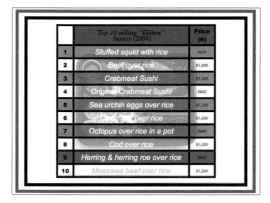

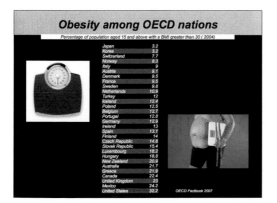

Is the Nonessential Always "Noise"?

It is generally true that unnecessary elements decrease a design's efficiency and increase the possibility of unintended consequences. But does this mean that we must remove everything that is not absolutely essential to a design? Some say a minimalist approach is the most efficient. But efficiency itself is not necessarily an absolute good and not always the ideal approach.

When it comes to the display of quantitative information using charts, tables, graphs, etc., I strongly favor designs that include the highest SNR possible without adornment. I use a lot of photographs in my presentations, so when I do show a chart or a graph, I usually do not place other elements on the slide. There is nothing wrong with placing a bar chart, for example, over a background image (as long as there is proper contrast or salience), but I think the data itself (with a high SNR) can be a very powerful, memorable graphic on its own.

With other visuals, however, you may want to consider including or retaining elements that serve to support the message at a more emotional level. This may seem like a contradiction to the idea that "less is more." However, emotional elements often do matter—sometimes, they matter a lot. Clarity should be your guiding principle. As with all things, balance is important and the use of emotional elements depends on your particular circumstance, audience, and objectives. In the end, SNR is one principle among many to consider when creating visual messages.

ABOVE *The top slide is simple with its slightly textured background. The last three slides contain more nonessential elements that make them more interesting, but do not necessarily increase the clarity of the data. Any of the designs may be appropriate, however, depending on the situation.*

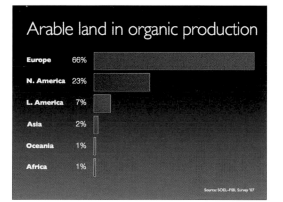

A simple bar chart without an image.

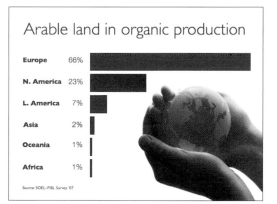

The same simple data with an image added. The image complements the underlining theme— saving the planet— without getting in the way of the chart. (Embedded background images on this page and opposite page from iStockphoto.com.)

2D or Not 2D? (That Is the Question)

Many design tools in Keynote and PowerPoint are quite useful, but the 3D tool is one I could very well do without. Taking 2D data and creating a 3D chart does not simplify it. The idea is that 3D may add emotion, but when it comes to charts and graphs, you should aim for simple, clean, and 2D (for 2D data). In *The Zen of Creativity* (Ballantine Books), author John Daido Loori says that the Zen aesthetic "reflects a simplicity that allows our attention to be drawn to that which is essential, stripping away the extra."

What is essential and what is extra is up to you, but stripping away the extra ink that 3D charts introduce seems like a good place to start. A 3D representation of 2D data increases what Edward Tufte calls the "ratio of ink-to-data." While it's nice to have a choice, 2D charts and graphs are almost always a better solution. Three-dimensional charts appear less accurate and can be difficult to comprehend. In addition, the viewing angle of 3D charts often makes it hard to see where the data points sit on an axis. If you do use 3D charts, avoid extreme perspectives.

The slides on the left are examples of 3D effects that compromise the display of very simple data. The slides on the right are suggested improvements.

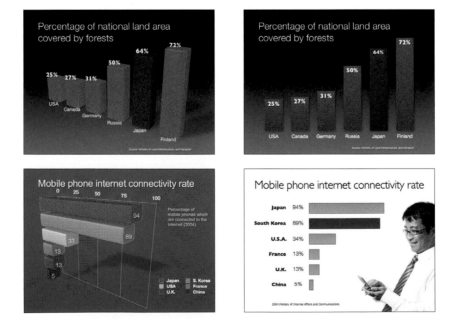

Who Says Your Logo Should Be on Every Slide?

"Branding" is one of the most overused and misunderstood terms in use today. Many people confuse the myriad elements of brand identity with brand or branding. The meaning of brand and branding goes far deeper than simply making one's logo as recognizable as possible. If you are presenting for an organization, try removing its logo from all but the first and last slide. If you want people to learn something and remember you, then make a good, honest presentation. The logo won't help close a sale or make a point, but it will create clutter and make the presentation visuals look like a commercial. We don't begin every new sentence in a conversation by restating our names, so why would you bombard people with your company logo on every slide?

Most companies that provide a PowerPoint template insist that employees use their logo on every slide. But is this good advice? Slide real estate is limited as it is, so don't clutter it with logos, trademarks, footers, and so on.

Tom Grimes, a Kansas State University journalism professor, offers this valuable advice when speaking about his research on the influence of on-screen clutter on understanding or retention.

> *"[I]f you want people to understand better, then get that stuff off the screen.... Clean it up and get it off because it is simply making it more difficult for people to understand what [you are] saying."*

Grimes is actually talking about the overpowering visual clutter found in TV newscasts, yet his advice is good for our multimedia presentations as well. Over the past several years, many TV news broadcasts have substituted pizzazz and sizzle—not to mention conjecture, speculation, and sensationalism—for clean, clear messages. Perhaps the visual clutter found in most TV news broadcasts has spilled over into corporate slide templates. One thing is for certain: if you want people to understand your visual messages, the answer is not to add more clutter but to remove it all.

A Few Points About Bullet Points

The "traditional way" of doing presentations with slides full of bulleted lists has been going on for so long that it has become part of corporate culture. It is simply "the way things are done." In Japan, for example, young employees entering a company are taught that when they create presentations with slideware they should put a minimum amount of text in each slide. This sounds like good advice, right? But, a "minimum" means something like six or seven lines of abbreviated text and figures along with several complete sentences. The idea of having one or two words—or (gasp!) no words—would be a sign of someone who did not do their homework. A series of text-filled slides with plenty of charts or tables shows that you are a "serious employee." Never mind that the audience can't really see the detail in the slides well (or that the executive board does not really understand your charts). If it looks complicated, it must be "good."

I have a shelf full of presentation books in English and Japanese. All of them say "use a minimum of text." Most of them define "minimum" as being anywhere from five to eight lines of bullet points. Presenters often learn the "1-7-7 Rule," which proves that conventional wisdom is out of sync. Here's the rub: Nobody can do a good presentation with slide after slide of bullet points. Nobody. Bullet points work well when used sparingly in documents to help readers scan content or summarize key points. But bullet points are usually not effective in a live talk.

The 1-7-7 Rule: What is it?

- Have only <u>one</u> main idea per slide
- Insert only <u>seven</u> lines of text maximum.
- Use only <u>seven</u> words per line maximum.
- The question is though: Does this work?
- Is this method really good advice?
- Is this really an appropriate, effective "visual"?
- This slide has just seven bullet points!

The presocom company   "Great slides R easy!"   November 15, 2007

How Many Bullets Points Per Slide?

A good general guideline is to use bullet points very rarely and only after careful consideration of other options for displaying the information in a way that best supports your message. Do not let the default bulleted lists of the software template dictate your decision. Sometimes bullet points may be the best choice. For example, if you are summarizing key specifications of a new product or reviewing the steps in a process, a clear bulleted or numbered list may be appropriate (depending, as always, on your content, objectives, and audience). People will tire quickly, however, if you show slides of bulleted lists, one after another, so use them with caution. I am not suggesting that you completely abandon the use of bullet points in multimedia presentations, but the usage should be a rare exception.

Remember these six aptitudes:

- Not just function but also DESIGN
- Not just argument but also STORY
- Not just focus but also SYMPHONY
- Not just logic but also EMPATHY
- Not just seriousness but also PLAY
- Not just accumulation but also MEANING

DESIGN — not only function
STORY — not only argument
SYMPHONY — not only focus
EMPATHY — not only logic
PLAY — not only seriousness
MEANING — not only accumulation

TOP *The blue slide was my first attempt to summarize the key points from Dan Pink's book* A Whole New Mind *in one slide.*

BOTTOM *The second slide uses about half the text to summarize the key points in a more engaging, visual way.*

Picture Superiority Effect

According to the picture superiority effect, pictures are remembered better than words—especially when people are casually exposed to the information and the exposure is for a very limited time. When information recall is measured just after exposure to a series of pictures or a series of words, the recall for pictures and words is about equal. The picture superiority effect, however, applies when the time after exposure is more than 30 seconds, according to research cited in *Universal Principles of Design* (Rockport Publishers). "Use the picture superiority effect to improve the recognition and recall of key information. Use pictures and words together, and ensure that they reinforce the same information for optimal effect," say authors Lidwell, Holden, and Butler. The effect is strongest when the pictures represent common, concrete things.

You can see the picture superiority effect used widely in marketing communications, such as posters, billboards, brochures, annual reports, etc. Keep this effect in mind, too, when designing slides with images and text that support a narrative. Visual imagery is a powerful mnemonic tool that helps learning and increases retention compared to, say, witnessing someone read words off a screen.

Going Visual

Images are a powerful and natural way for humans to communicate. The key word here is *natural*. We are hardwired for understanding images and using them to communicate. Something inside of us—even from a very young age—seems to yearn to draw, paint, photograph, or otherwise show the ideas in our heads.

In 2005, Alexis Gerard and Bob Goldstein published *Going Visual: Using Images to Enhance Productivity, Decision-Making and Profits* (Wiley). Gerard and Goldstein urge us to use visuals to tell a story or prove a point. However, the authors do not suggest using imaging technology because it is "cool" or "modern." Going visual is about using images to improve communication and business. For example, you could write about or talk about how a recent fire impacted production—but wouldn't it be far more powerful to send pictures with a smaller amount of text (or spoken words) to describe the situation? What would be more memorable? Which would have more impact?

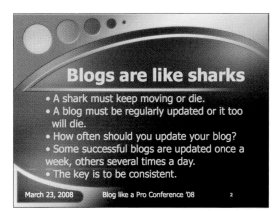

A traditional slide that duplicates the presenter's words is more of a reading test than a visual.

This slide does a much better job of enhancing the presenter's spoken words. The photo has impact and makes the point clearly. Which slide is more memorable? Plus, since people are not reading, they can actually listen to you. (Photo of shark from iStockphoto.com.)

Using images is an efficient way to compare and contrast changes, such as the effects of drought in this simulated example. (The original embedded image of the dry lake bed from iStockphoto.com.)

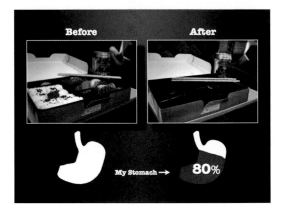

This tongue-in-cheek example shows the actual bento mentioned in Chapter 1 as the genesis for this book. Before-and-after and then-and-now visual comparisons are easy to create and remember. Al Gore used many then-and-now visual comparisons in his presentations and in the movie An Inconvenient Truth *to show physical changes over time.*

Ask yourself this: What information are you representing with the written word on a slide that you could replace with a photograph (or other appropriate image or graphic)? You still need text for labeling and other things. But if you are using text on a slide for describing something, you probably could use an image more effectively.

Images are powerful, efficient, and direct. Images can also be used very effectively as mnemonic devices to make messages more memorable. If people cannot listen and read at the same time, why do most presentation slides contain far more words than images? One reason, historically, is that businesspeople have been limited by technology. Visual communication and technology go hand in hand. Today, however, most people do have the basic tools available—for example, digital cameras and editing software—for easy-to-place, high-quality images in presentations.

No more excuses. It just takes a different way of looking at presentations. It takes the realization that modern presentations with slides and other multimedia have more in common with cinema (images and narration) and comics (images and text) than they do with written documents. Today's presentations increasingly share more in common with a documentary film than an overhead transparency.

On the following pages you will see a few slides that demonstrate different visual treatments in support of a single message. The context is a presentation on gender and labor issues in Japan. The purpose of the slides was to support visually the claim that "72% of the part-time workers in Japan are women." This statistic is from the Japanese Ministry of Labor. The presenter wanted the audience members to remember the 72% figure as it was discussed again in the presentation. So we designed a subtle, simple, memorable slide that fit into an appealing and attractive theme.

The original slide showcases various problems: the clip art does not reinforce the simple statistic, nor does it fit the theme of women in the Japanese labor market; the background is a tired, overused PowerPoint template; and the text is difficult to read.

While the text on this slide is easy to read and the clip art is a bit more appropriate to the subject, it still does not give the slide a strong visual impact or a professional look and feel.

This slide displays the same information in a typical pie chart. The chart's 3D effects and extra lines, however, do not improve the impact or readability of the information.

In this case, the two bullet points are easy to read in an instant. The photo of an actual female part-time worker in Japan is a step in the right direction, but it could still be much better.

ABOVE *The four slides above are different treatments of the message communicated in the slides on the previous page. All these slides would nicely complement the presenter's narration. (Notice that the two slides without the word "Japan" would be virtually meaningless without the presenter's narration.)*

BELOW *The final slide design used in the presentation is shown on the left. The remaining slides in the deck were then redesigned using Japanese stock images to give the entire presentation a consistent visual theme that supported the presenter's words.*

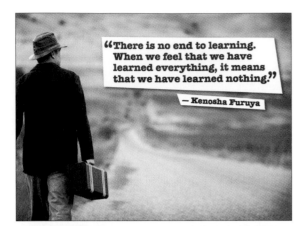

All the slides on this page use images that bleed off the edge, filling the entire screen, and the text and images work in harmony. The masking tape and paper note shown below is a JPEG image from iStockphoto that provides an interesting effect and prevents the text from getting lost in the background. This element provides good contrast with the text and adds depth to the overall visual. The slight angle of the note and text add interest without being distracting.

Slide images on this page from iStockphoto.com.

The slides on this page are from the portfolio of Jeff Brenman, the creator of Apollo Ideas and the winner of SlideShare's "World's Best Presentation Contest" in 2007. (You can see the slide deck that won him first place in the next chapter.) Jeff has a talent for combining images and text in a way that is fresh and effective for augmenting the presenter's messages.

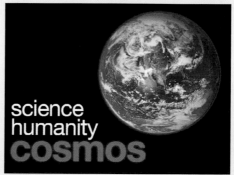

Where Can You Get Good Images?

Getty Images may have the best quality and the greatest selection of images for presentations. But what if you cannot afford to make a slide presentation that costs hundreds or thousands of dollars in stock image fees? In that case, low-cost, royalty-free "micro-stock" images are a good alternative. The site I recommend most often is iStockphoto.com (the source of most of the images used in this book). The iStockphoto library is incredibly easy to use; after performing a search, you can just roll over thumbnails for a larger view without having to open another page.

I do not suggest that you limit your image searches to iStockphoto.com. I subscribe to other photo sites and use photos I shoot myself more and more. But when it comes to great micro-stock, iStockphoto is the best. They have millions of images from which to choose and add thousands of images every week. The site just keeps getting better and better. Plus, iStockphoto has a "free image of the week" so you may want to check back from time to time to see what's new—and free. At the back of this book, you will find a special code, just for you, that entitles you to 10 free photos on the iStockphoto website. So take your free credits and download a few images from iStockphoto.com.

My personal favorite photo site
• iStockphoto (www.istockphoto.com)

Other places to get low-cost images
• Dreams Time (www.dreamstime.com)
• Fotolia (www.fotolia.com)
• Japanese Streets (www.japanesestreets.com)
• Shutter Stock (www.shutterstock.com)

A few sites that offer free images
• Morgue File (www.morguefile.com)
• Flickr Creative Commons Pool (www.flickr.com/creativecommons)
• Everystockphoto search engine (www.everystockphoto.com)
• NASA Image Exchange (http://nix.nasa.gov); these images are generally not copyrighted, but read the copyright for each image to be sure

Quote This

While long bullet points are not very effective visually, displaying quotations in slides can be a very powerful technique. Depending on the presentation, I often use quite a few quotes from various fields to support my points. The trick is not to use them too much and to make sure they are short and legible.

When I first saw Tom Peters give a live presentation a few years ago while I was working in Silicon Valley, I was happy to see that he used a good deal of quotes from various experts, authors, and industry leaders. Using quotes in his presentation visuals is a big deal for Tom. In fact, it is No. 18 on his "Presentation Excellence 56" article on his website.

To explain why he uses so many quotes, Tom says:

> *"My conclusions are much more credible when I back them up with Great Sources. I say pretty radical stuff. I say 'Get radical!' That's one thing. But then I show a quote from Jack Welch, who, after all, ran a $150 billion company (I didn't): 'You can't behave in a calm, rational manner; you've got to be out there on the lunatic fringe.' Suddenly my radicalism is 'certified' by a 'real operator.' Also, I find that people like to get beyond the spoken word, and see a SIMPLE reminder of what I'm saying."*

Quotes can indeed add credibility to your story. Weave a simple quote into your narrative to support your point, or as a springboard from which you can launch your next topic. Remember, quotes should be short, in most cases, since it can become quite tedious to have a presenter read a paragraph from a screen.

Text Within Images

I almost always use quotes that are straight out of material I have read or from personal interviews. My books, for example, are filled with sticky notes and pages full of my comments and highlighter marks. I sketch a star and write a note to myself next to great passages for future reference. It's kind of messy, but it works for me when I put presentations together.

When I use a quote, I sometimes add a graphic element that targets people's emotions, creates more visual interest, and enhances the effect of the slide. But rather than using a small photo or other element, consider placing the text within a larger photo. To do this, you will want to use an image at least as large as your slide dimensions (800x600, for example) for your background. Look for an image that supports the point you are making with the quotation. The image should have plenty of empty space so the text fits comfortably with good contrast.

This page shows two slides that display a quotation in a typical manner. On the opposite page, you'll see the same quote displayed *within* the image rather than simply next to a smaller version of the image. Notice the difference in the visual impact of both the quote and image.

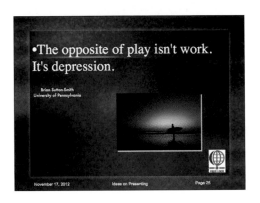

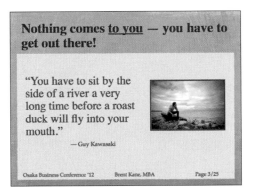

(Photos in these slides from iStockphoto.com.)

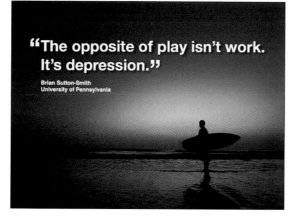

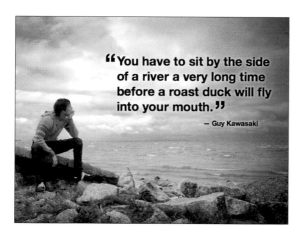

A white background is placed behind the text as if it were a piece of paper. This helps the text pop out from the background, making it easier to read and giving it a more analog texture .

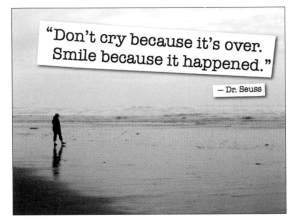

Here, a photo of the person being quoted helps enliven the text. Note that Kakuzo-san is gazing toward the quote.

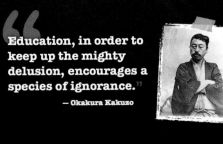

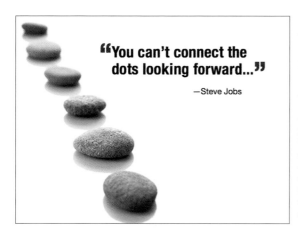

"You can't connect the dots looking forward..."

—Steve Jobs

This quote is presented over two slides. The text on the second slide is rather long, but the key phrase is highlighted in red. You do not want to use too many visuals with long quotes like this. However, if you introduce them only occasionally, and you do not rush through the quote, longer quotes can be useful for providing context. Note that the type is large enough to be seen from the back of the room. Most people may not read the text onscreen—they may just listen to you. Nonetheless, type that is too small to read is maddening to audience members.

"...you can only connect them looking backwards. So you have to trust that the dots will somehow connect in your future. You have to trust in something — your gut, destiny, life, karma, whatever...it has made all the difference in my life."

—Steve Jobs

Creating Bilingual Visuals

Combining languages on a slide can be effective—as long as the text is in different sizes. One language needs to be visually subordinate to the other. When I present in Japanese, the Japanese text is larger than the English text (but in a way that creates a harmonious fit). If my talk is in English, the English text is larger. When text from both languages is the same size, it creates visual discord as the type elements compete with each other for attention. The technique of placing text from one language in a clearly dominant position is commonly used in signage for public transportation and in advertising. On general principle, we need to keep text to a minimum in visuals; when creating bilingual slides, we have to be extra careful with limiting the text. Samples from my own presentations appear on the opposite page.

The technique of placing text from one language in a clearly dominant position is commonly used in signage for public transportation and in advertising.

In the first example on the left, all the text is very close to the same size and color. In the second example, the Japanese text is subordinate. Which is easier to scan in an instant?

Emptiness which is conceptually liable to be mistaken for sheer nothingness is in fact the reservoir of infinite possibilities.

— Daisetz T. Suzuki

Empty Space

Empty space, also called negative space or white space, is a concept that is supremely simple, yet the most difficult for people to apply. Whether designing a document or slide, the urge to fill empty areas with more elements is just too great. One of the biggest mistakes typical businesspeople make with presentation slides (and documents) is going out of their way to seemingly use every centimeter of space, filling it with text, boxes, clip art, charts, footers, and the ubiquitous company logo.

Empty space implies elegance and clarity. This is true with graphic design, but you can see the importance of space (both visual and physical) in the context of, say, interior design as well. High-end brand shops are always designed to create as much open space as possible. Empty space can convey a feeling of high quality, sophistication, and importance.

Empty space has a purpose. But those new to design may only see the positive elements, such as text or a graphic, without ever "seeing" the empty space and using that space to make the design more compelling. It is the empty space that gives a design air and lets the positive elements breathe. If it was true that empty space in a design is "wasted space," then it would make sense to remove such waste. However, empty space in a design is not "nothing." It is, indeed, a powerful "something," which gives the few elements on your slide their power.

In the Zen arts, you will find an appreciation for empty space. A painting, for example, may be mostly "empty" except for two to three elements, but the placement of the elements within that space forms a powerful message. You can apply the same approach to a room. Many Japanese homes have a *washitsu*, a traditional room with tatami mats, that is simple and mostly empty. The empty space allows for the appreciation of a single item, such as a single flower or a single wall hanging. The emptiness is a powerful design element itself. In this case, the more we add, the more diluted and less effective the design of a graphic, slide, document, or living space, becomes.

Using Empty Space

The blue slide at top right is very typical, with several bullet points and an image related to the topic. Rather than making good use of empty space, the blue slide has trapped space in areas around the image. Instead of using one busy slide, I broke the flow of the content into six slides for the introduction of the "Hara hachi bu" concept. Since it is not necessary to put all the words spoken by the presenter on the slides, much of the onscreen text was removed. The slides have a clean white background with plenty of active empty space that helps guide viewers' eyes. When a new slide is revealed, the eyes are naturally drawn to the image first (it's larger, colorful) and then quickly go to the text element.

(Images in slides on this page from iStockphoto.com.)

The Power of Faces to Get Attention and Guide Viewers' Eyes

We are amazingly good at seeing faces. We are so good at spotting faces that we even see them where they do not exist. In fact, said Carl Sagan, "As an inadvertent side effect, the pattern-recognition machinery in our brains is so efficient in extracting a face from a clutter of other detail that we sometimes see faces where there are none." This explains why people see an image of Mother Teresa in a cheese sandwich or a face on Mars. Faces—and things approximating images of faces—get our attention. Graphic designers and marketers know this very well, which is why you so often see faces in various forms of marketing communication.

Photo: NASA

We are naturally drawn to look in the direction that other people are looking. I noticed that even my baby daughter looks where I look; this tendency starts at an early age.

Using images of faces—even nonhuman faces—can be effective for getting viewers' attention. This is especially true in mediums such as posters, magazines, and billboards, but this concept can be applied to multimedia and large screen displays as well. Because faces are so effective at getting attention, they must be used with discretion. One important consideration is the issue of eye gaze and leading the eye of the viewer. For example, the two images below are from a study by James Breeze at *usableworld.com.au,* which used eye-tracking software to determine if the direction the baby looked onscreen influenced the eye gaze of the readers. Not surprisingly, the text on the right got more attention from the eyes when the baby's eye gaze was in that direction.

An eye-tracking study by James Breeze shows the influence of eye gaze in guiding the viewer's eye on the page. Eye gaze in presentation visuals may have similar influences on the viewers' attention.

Whether you use images of people or animals in your visuals is up to you; each context and topic are different. However, if you do, be mindful of the power that images of faces have for getting attention and try to use eye gaze to help guide the viewer's eye.

If you use images of people, make sure they do not unintentionally guide viewers away from what you want them to see. For example, if a text element or chart is the highest priority, it is important to not have images of people looking in the opposite direction from those elements. How do the images in the slides shown here guide your eyes toward or away from the other elements? While either slide in each pair may be acceptable, notice how the slides on the right lead your eye to the text or chart.

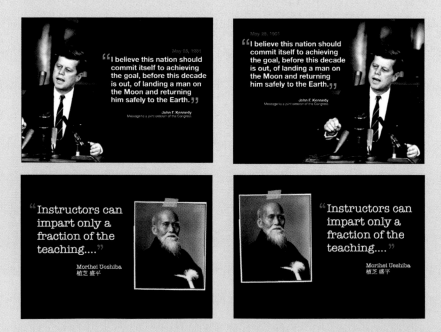

The effect of eye gaze is more obvious in this example. Many people who look at the image on the left report that they can almost feel their eyes being diverted off the slide. The sample on the right shows a much more harmonious fit between the image and the text.

Not only faces of humans that get your attention and lead the eye. In the sample on the left above, the bird is clearly looking in the direction of the type, his beak acting like a pointing finger. In the sample on the right, it is not the face of the bird as much as its orientation—flying up toward the type—that leads the eye like a soaring arrow.

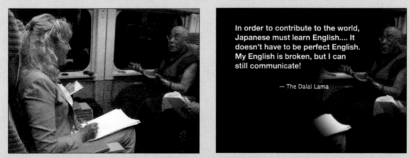

The slide on the left features an image of Judit Kawaguchi, a writer for the Japan Times, interviewing the Dalai Lama on the Bullet Train in Japan. The quote displayed in the second slide is from that actual interview on the train. The first slide shows the context, then the second slide fades in (dissolve transition), which results in Judit fading out and being replaced by the text. With this effect, the right third of the slide (the Dalai Lama) never appears to change.

Balance

Balance is important in a design, and one way to achieve good balance and clarity is through the intelligent use of empty space. A well-balanced design has a clear, single, unified message. A well-designed slide has a clear starting point and guides the viewer through the design. The viewer should never have to "think" about where to look. A visual must never confuse anyone. What are the most important, less important, and least important parts of the design need to be clearly expressed with a clear hierarchy and a good balance of display elements.

Through the careful placement of positive elements, empty space can be dynamic and active. The conscious use of empty space can even bring motion to your design. In this way, the empty space is not passive but active. If you want to bring a more dynamic feel and interest to your slide design, consider using an asymmetrical design. Asymmetrical designs activate empty space and make designs more interesting; they are more informal and dynamic, with a variety of sizes and shapes.

Symmetrical designs feature a strong emphasis along a central vertical axis. Symmetrical balance is vertically centered and equivalent on both sides. Symmetrical designs are more static than asymmetrical designs and evoke feelings of formality or stability. There is nothing wrong with centered, symmetrical designs, although empty space in such designs is generally passive and pushed to the side.

Design is about seeing and manipulating shapes, but if we do not see the empty space in a slide as a shape, then it will be ignored and any use of empty space will be accidental. Consequently, the results will not be as powerful. Good presentations will incorporate a series of presentation visuals that have a mix of slides that are symmetrical and asymmetrical.

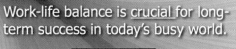

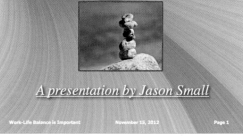

Both slides have good balance. The top slide is a common, symmetrical design that is not very interesting. The bottom slide is asymmetrical, creating a simpler yet more powerful visual. (Image from iStockphoto.com.)

One way to activate empty space and create a dynamic, asymmetrical slide is to use large images that bleed off the edge. Use the empty space to place small amounts of text or other elements. On the right is another Guy Kawasaki quote—one of my favorites—used in one of my branding talks in Japan. In the first slide, the quote is symmetrical. The other two slides are examples of asymmetrical designs.

(Images on slides above from iStockphoto.com.)

Grids and the Rule of Thirds

For centuries, artists and designers have introduced a proportion called the "golden mean" or "golden ratio" found in nature into their works. The golden section rectangle has a proportion of 1:1.618. There is a belief that we are naturally drawn to images that have proportions approaching the golden section rectangle, just as we are often drawn to things in the natural environment with golden-mean proportions. However, attempting to design visuals according to golden-mean proportions is impractical in most cases. But, the "rule of thirds," which is derived from the golden mean, is a basic design technique that can help you add balance (symmetrical or asymmetrical), beauty, and a higher aesthetic quality to your visuals.

The rule of thirds is a basic technique that photographers learn for framing their shots. Subjects placed exactly in the middle can often make for an uninteresting photo. A viewfinder can be divided by lines—real or just imagined—so that you have four intersecting lines or crossing points and nine boxes that resemble a tic-tac-toe board. These four crossing points (also called "power points," if you can believe it) are areas you might place your main subject, rather than in the center.

Remember, there is no liberty in absolute freedom when it comes to design. You need to limit your choices so that you do not waste time adjusting every single design element to a new position. I recommend that you create some sort of clean, simple grid to build your visuals upon. Although you may not be aware of it, virtually every Web page and every page in a book or magazine is built atop a grid. Grids can save you time and ensure that your design elements fit more harmoniously on the display. Using grids to divide your slide "canvas" into thirds, for example, is an easy way at least to approach golden-mean proportions. In addition, you can use the grids to align elements and give the overall design balance, a clear flow and point of focus, and a natural overall cohesiveness and aesthetic quality that is not accidental but is by design.

The image on the right is not a slide—it's a picture of Hokusai Katsushika's (1760–1849) "Red Fuji" from the ukiyo-e series called Thirty-six Views of Mount Fuji. I placed a nine-panel grid over the print to show how the rule of thirds can be seen in the composition. Remember, however, that the rule of thirds is not a rule at all, it is only a guideline. But it is a very useful guideline when you are aiming to achieve a balanced yet asymmetrical look.

Below are a few examples of presentation visuals designed by either using a nine-panel grid or by just keeping the rule of thirds in mind while placing and cropping the photos and arranging elements. You'll also notice that the images themselves have pretty good rule of thirds proportions. The iStockphoto images used here were chosen in part based on the photo's proportions and how the image guides the eye and offers empty space for the design elements.

Hokusai's "Red Fuji" with nine-panel grid laid on top.

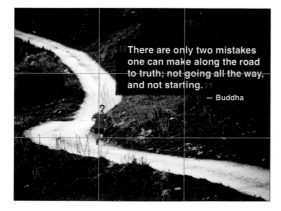

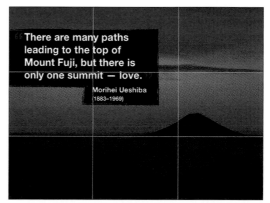

Create your own visual style. Let it be unique for yourself and yet identifiable for others.

— Orson Welles

The Big Four: Contrast, Repetition, Alignment, Proximity

These four principles—contrast, repetition, alignment, and proximity—are not all there is to know about graphic design. But, understanding these simple, related concepts and applying them to slide design can make for far more satisfying and effective designs.

Contrast

Contrast simply means difference. And for whatever reason, we are all wired to notice differences—perhaps our brains think they are still back in the savannah scanning for wild predators. We are not conscious of it, but we are scanning and looking for similarities and differences all the time. Contrast is what we notice, and it's what gives a design its energy. So you should make elements that are not the same clearly different, not just slightly different.

Contrast is one of the most powerful design concepts because, really, any design element can be contrasted with another. You can achieve contrast in many ways—for example, through the manipulation of space (near and far, empty and filled), through color choices (dark and light, cool and warm), by typeface selection (serif and sans serif, bold and narrow), by the positioning of elements (top and bottom, isolated and grouped), and so on.

Making use of contrast can help you create a design in which one item is clearly dominant. This helps the viewer "get" the point of your design quickly. Every good design has a strong and clear focal point, so it helps to have clear contrast among elements, with one element being clearly dominant. If all items in a design are of equal or similar weight with weak contrast and nothing clearly dominant, it is difficult for the viewer to know where to look. Designs with strong contrast attract interest and help the viewer make sense of the visual. Weak contrast is not only boring, but it can be confusing.

Every single element of a design—such as line, shape, color, texture, size, space, and type—can be manipulated to create contrast. The next page compares slides that make good use of contrast to slides with weaker contrast.

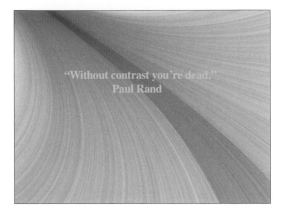

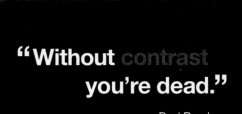

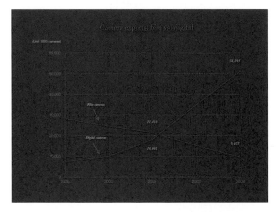

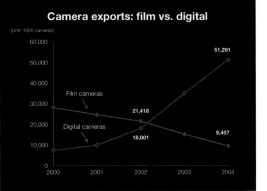

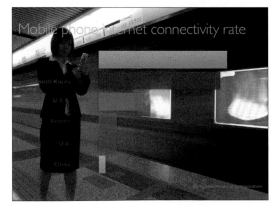

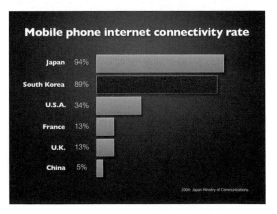

Repetition

The principle of repetition simply means the reuse of the same or similar elements throughout a design. Repetition of certain design elements in a slide or among a deck of slides will bring a clear sense of unity, consistency, and cohesiveness. Where contrast is about showing differences, repetition is about subtly using elements to make sure a design is viewed as part of a larger whole. If you use a stock template from your software application, then repetition is already built into your slides. For example, a consistent background and consistent use of type adds unity across a deck of slides.

However, you must be careful not to have too much repetition among slides. Most of the built-in templates have been seen many times before and may not suit your unique situation. Many of the standard templates also have background elements that soon become tiring and make it difficult to distinguish between slides. For example, let's say you use a starfish image in the lower right corner of slides for a presentation on marine biology. To make the starfish a stronger repetitive element, vary its size and location occasionally and in harmony with the content of the different slides (but in a subtle way that does not interfere with the primary message).

The slides on the next page show good examples of repetition. For his presentation on the process of designing a book, Swiss designer and photographer Markuz Wernli Saito used his own full bleed photos for all his slides. To help give the entire presentation a unified look, he used a similar red note and paperclip to "hold" the text in each slide. While he varied the placement and size of the note and paperclip image, the consistent use of the element and the red color gave his visuals a professional and unified look.

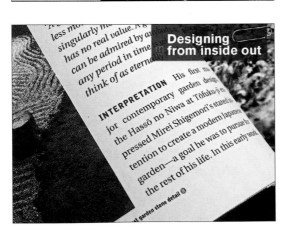

Alignment

The whole point of the alignment principle is that nothing in your slide design should look like random placement. Every element is connected visually via an invisible line. Where repetition is more concerned with elements across a deck of slides, alignment is about obtaining unity among elements of a single slide. Even elements that are quite far apart on a slide should have a visual connection, something that is easier to achieve with the use of grids. When you place elements on a slide, try to align them with an existing element.

Many people fail to apply the alignment principle, which often results in elements being almost—but not quite—aligned. This may not seem like a big deal, but these kinds of slides look less sophisticated and less professional overall. The audience may not be conscious of it, but slides that contain elements in alignment look cleaner. And, assuming other principles are applied harmoniously as well, slides with aligned elements should be easier to understand quickly.

Proximity

The principle of proximity is about moving things closer or farther apart to achieve a more organized look. The principle says that related items should be grouped together so they will be viewed as a group, rather than as several unrelated elements. Viewers will assume that items that are not near each other are not closely related. They will naturally tend to group similar items that are close to each other into a single unit.

Audience members should never have to "work" at trying to figure out which caption goes with which graphic or whether a line of text is a subtitle or a line of unrelated text. Do not make audiences think. That is, do not make them "think" about the wrong stuff, like trying to decipher your slide's organization and design priority. A slide is not a page in a book or magazine, so you are not going to have more than a few elements or groups of elements. In her best-selling book *The Non-Designer's Design Book* (Peachpit Press), Robin Williams says that we must be conscious of where our eye goes first when we step back and look at our design. When you look at your slide, notice where your eye is drawn first, second, and so on. What path does your eye take?

This title slide lacks a design priority. Due to the poor use of alignment and proximity, the slide seems to contain five different elements.

Principles of Presentation Design:

Tips on how to think like a designer

By Less Nessman

Director of the PRKW Institute

This slide uses symmetrical balance and better proximity, with related items now clearly together. Greater contrast is achieved by adjusting the type size and color to give the design a clear priority.

Principles of Presentation Design
Tips on how to think like a designer

Less Nessman
Director PRKW Institute

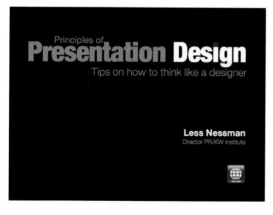

These two slides show how aligning all elements flush right creates a strong invisible line that ties all the elements together in a way that is more interesting than the more common symmetrical title. The type and color are also adjusted to create greater contrast and interest. The red dot in the title ties in with the red logo at the bottom.

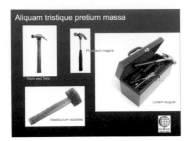

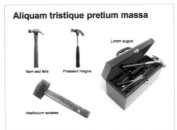

The slide on the left looks busier due to the abrupt contrast between the background color of the images. By aligning the text and photos and making the image backgrounds transparent (in this case, by simply changing the slide background to white) the slide is much cleaner and noise is reduced.

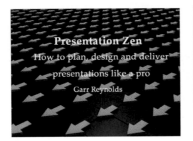

In the slide on the left, the background image has too much salience, making the title hard to see. Choosing a more appropriate background image that allows the text to remain clearly in the foreground and grouping the text lines makes for a stronger title slide.

By making the background of the fish photo seem transparent in the slide on the left, the image and text blend together harmoniously into a more unified visual. To make an image seem transparent, you can often simply change the slide background to white.

The slide on the left uses a busy template that makes the useful area of the slide about one-third smaller. The slide on the right covers the entire slide with the image. The text is clearly in the foreground while the image serves both as background and foreground, making the overall visual dynamic and unified with a cleaner, more dramatic look.

(Images on this page and opposite page from iStockphoto.com.)

This slide features a typical graph exported from Excel. It is impossible to identify the countries as the text is too small and at an angle. The primary problem is that this is too much data to display. This amount of information would be better presented in a handout.

The text and data are easier to see when the contrast between the foreground and background is improved. Including only key variables allows for larger bars and figures. Information on excluded variables can be distributed in a handout.

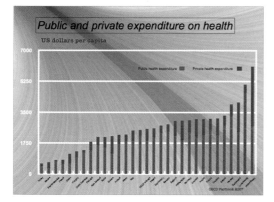

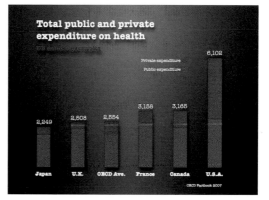

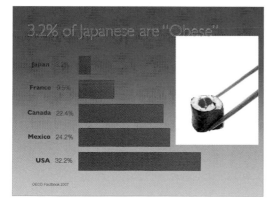

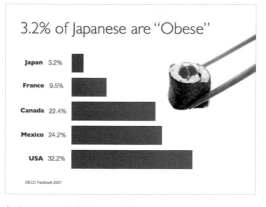

Here, the background color is not only a poor fit with the colors of the bars, but it does not provide enough contrast and makes the text hard to read. The white background on the sushi photo adds unnecessary noise to the visual.

In this revision, the background of the sushi photo "disappears" to match the white background of the slide. The text, bars, and background feature much better contrast and are easier to read.

This kind of slide is not unusual but suffers from typical problems such as a generic title, underlined text, and a small graphic that does not amplify the message of the presenter. Yellow text on this kind of blue background has been seen a million times before.

Here the same message as the slide on the left is made but the visual is big and bold and shows the trash problem in a way that illustrates and amplifies the presenter's story in a more visceral way. The type is gritty and the highlight color (green) subtly matches the tone of green of the plastic bottles.

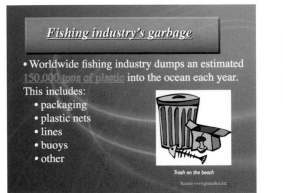

The quote and the photo are epic, yet this slide lacks impact or drama. The background looks very template-like and is too busy, making text hard to read. The type is a mess with the quote appearing as two bullet points. All elements are centered on the slide which results in trapped space. Even though there are few elements, the slide appears cluttered.

The type is clean and large. The photo is large and makes an impact, taking up the right third of the slide and bleeding off the edge. Distracting background elements of the photo are removed. JFK's sight line is in the direction of the quote. Most viewers' eyes will go naturally to the face first and then smoothly to the type.

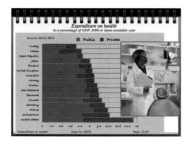

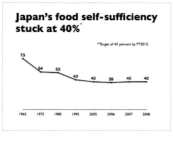

Keeping the principle of Signal vs. Noise in mind, it's easy to see that the various and hard-to-read fonts, unnecessary lines, and decorative elements on the slide on the left make for a lot of noise. By removing those elements and making a better headline, the signal is enhanced.

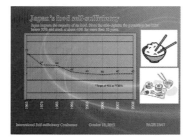

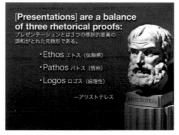

The slide on the left is a rather typical PowerPoint slide of yesteryear. The slide on the right strips away the nonessential, revealing a very simple point that will be understood in an instant. Then people can spend their time discussing what the data mean rather than being distracted by a decorative data slide.

The slide on the left uses too many colors, a tiny graphic, and poor use of type, including underlined text. On the right the visual has more impact, the colors are toned way down, and the mix of English and Japanese is presented in a cleaner, more harmonious fashion.

The slide on the left looks amateurish and does not match the feeling of the Japanese proverb. The slide on the right makes good use of empty space, the shade of brown for the quotation marks is the same as the fur of the monkey, and the English and Japanese work in better harmony by having them set in different sizes. The monkey is also moving in the direction of the type.

(Images on this page and opposite page from iStockphoto.com.)

The more strikingly visual your presentation is, the more people will remember it. And more importantly, they will remember you.

— Paul Arden

In Sum

- Design matters. But design is not about decoration or ornamentation. Design is about making communication as easy and clear for the viewer as possible.

- Keep the principle of signal-to-noise ratio in mind to remove all nonessential elements. Remove visual clutter. Avoid 3D effects.

- People remember visuals better than bullet points. Always ask yourself how you can use a strong visual—including quantitative displays—to enhance your narrative.

- Empty space is not nothing; it is a powerful something. Learn to see and manipulate empty space to give your slide designs greater organization, clarity, and interest.

- Use high-quality photos that make an impact and are easily seen and understood. Consider using full-bleed images and place type elements on top in the simplest, most balanced arrangement possible.

- Use the principle of contrast to create strong dynamic differences among elements that are different. If it is different, make it *very* different.

- Use the principle of repetition to repeat selected elements throughout your slides. This can help give your slides unity and organization.

- Use the principle of alignment to visually connect elements on a slide. Invisible gridlines are very useful for achieving good alignment. Using a grid gives your slides a clean, well-organized look.

- Use the principle of proximity to ensure that related items are grouped together. People tend to interpret items together or near to each other as belonging to the same group.

Sample Visuals: Images & Text

In this chapter you can review slides from several presenters who often make presentations in the "real world." (Because of limited space, only a small number of slides are shown from each presentation.) The sample slides are not all necessarily perfect. However, while we can judge a slide in terms of its adherence to basic design principles, it is difficult to judge the effectiveness of its design without seeing how the visuals are used in the live talk.

Although the content and circumstances are different in each case, what the slides shown in this chapter have in common is that they are simple, highly visual, and served (or could serve) a successful supportive role in a live talk. These slides augment the presenter's narrative and help make things clear.

Your visuals should be engaging and "part of the show," but they must also be easy to understand—quickly. If you need to explain something complex, then build (animate) the parts of your chart or diagram in logical and clear steps. Simplicity, restraint, and harmony are important considerations when designing slides and other multimedia. The primary goal is not to make slides look good. The goal is clarity. However, if you design slides while always mindful of the principles of simplicity and restraint—as well as the basic design concepts outlined in Chapter 6—your slides will indeed look attractive.

Be Like Bamboo

I created the slides shown on the next three pages for my 12-minute presentation at TEDxTokyo. During this fast-paced talk, I shared my thoughts on the lessons we can learn from observing the world around us. Even the humble bamboo, which plays such an integral role in Japanese culture, offers lessons in simplicity, flexibility, and resilience. I made the slide background from composites of simulated washi paper to give the visuals a more earthy, textured look. The aspect ratio of the slides is 16:9 to match the wide screen at the venue in Tokyo. You can find all the slides used in this presentation on Slideshare.net:

www.slideshare.net/garr

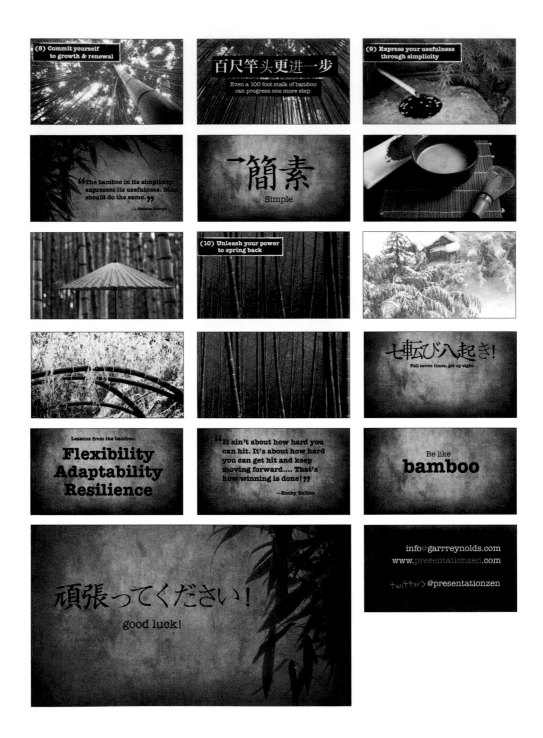

Think Like a Designer

I created these slides quickly and simply with nothing but type and a background. I use these for a 90-minute session introducing basic design concepts to non-designers. Mostly, this session is a back-and-forth discussion with the slides displayed onscreen to simply keep us on track and give structure to the session. I use the whiteboard and handouts to highlight examples for each of the key messages.

Differentiation

Here you can see the first 34 slides (out of more than 100) for my presentation on the issue of branding and transformation. The client—a major international financial firm—asked me to focus on differentiation and engagement. The 35-minute presentation also featured a few short video clips to underscore my points. As I spoke, the slides appeared behind me on a huge backlit screen, at which I rarely glanced. Some of the slides contained quotes and visual examples of what I was talking about. But most of all, I had a point, and I had stories and examples to illustrate that point. The slides provided an important and supportive backdrop that amplified my message.

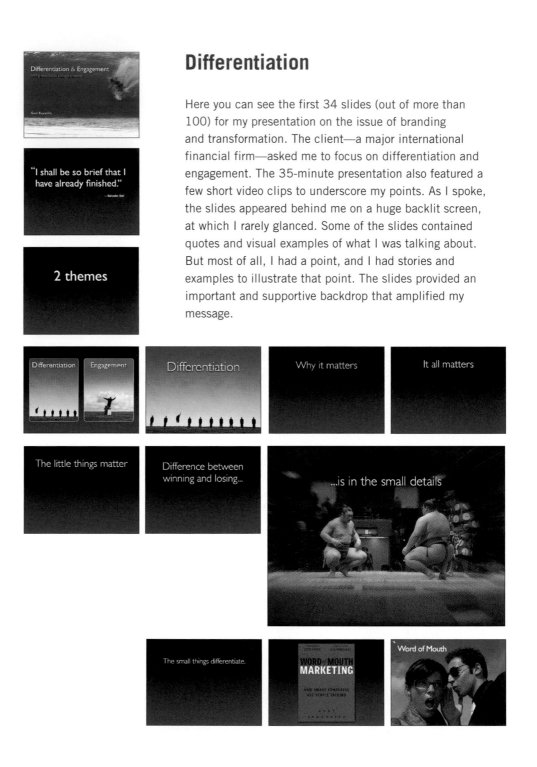

Shift Happens*

Jeff Brenman
Founder and CEO, Apollo Ideas
www.apolloideas.com

The slides for this presentation are a stylized version of a slideshow originally created by Karl Fisch to examine globalization and America's future in the 21st century. It's designed for online viewing; in a live talk, however, some of the text could be removed to make the slides a better complement to the speaker's words. You can find all the slides used in this presentation on Slideshare.net:

www.slideshare.net/jbrenman

You can see an official update to the original Shift Happens video presentation from Karl Fisch and Scott McLeod on Wikispaces.com:

www.shifthappens.wikispaces.com

*First Prize, Slideshare's World's Best Presentation Contest (2007).

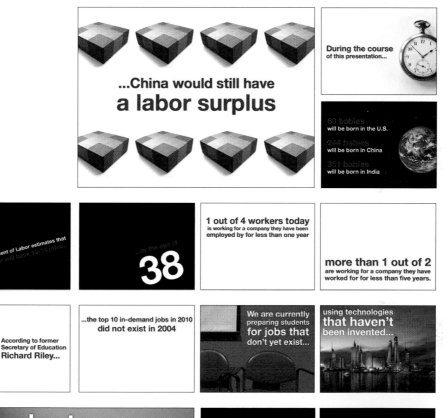

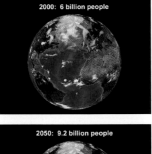

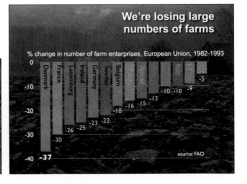

The Sustainable Food Lab*

Chris Landry
Director of Development & Communications,
Sustainable Food Laboratory
www.sustainablefoodlab.org

The slides shown here are part of a modified slide deck Chris Landry uses for talks about his organization and the work it does to bring more sustainability to mainstream food systems. Chris added a bit more text to these slides so they make a little more sense when viewed without narration in printed form, but the visuals were originally created to augment his live talk. You can find all the slides used in this presentation on Slideshare.net:

www.slideshare.net/chrislandry

Third Prize, Slideshare's World's Best Presentation Contest (2007).

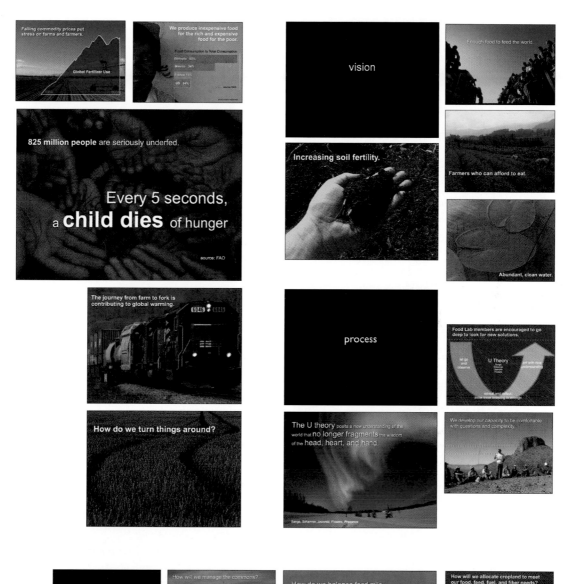

Aromatic Chemistry

Dr. Aisyah Saad Abdul Rahim

*Lecturer in Pharmaceutical Chemistry,
School of Pharmaceutical Sciences
Universiti Sains Malaysia*

www.pha.usm.my/pharmacy/Aisyah2006.htm

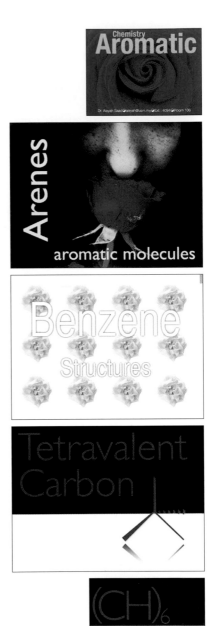

The visuals shown here are typical of the lecture slides Dr. Saad uses in her Pharmaceutical Chemistry classes in Malaysia. These slides are samples from her lecture on "Aromatic Chemistry." The black-and-red slides serve as a historical introduction to benzene while the second group illustrates the four essential features of aromatic compounds.

"I teach 'Aromatic Chemistry' to pharmacy students," says Dr. Saad. "Mindful of Asian students' penchant towards rote learning, I decided to apply the Presentation Zen approach in my lectures. The first few lectures had the students baffled because they could hardly jot down any notes. Later, they figured out that they had to pay more attention to my lectures. I use the Presentation Zen approach because it appeals to me visually and provides an amazing way to make students listen and understand more in lectures rather than just copying down notes off my slides."

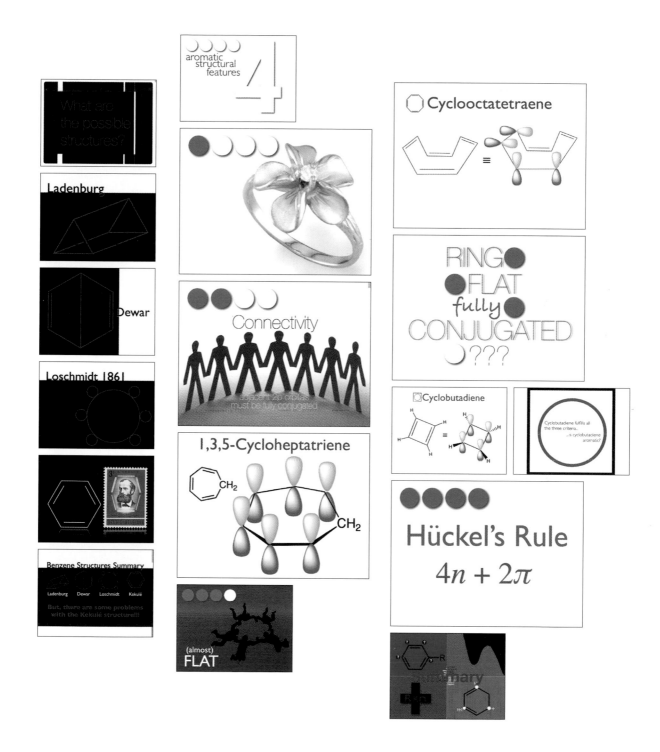

Presenting on Animal-Based Issues

Sangeeta Kumar, M.Ed.
Education Coordinator,
People for the Ethical Treatment of Animals
www.peta.org

In her position as education coordinator for People for the Ethical Treatment of Animals, Sangeeta Kumar travels a lot and gives highly visual presentations on animal-based issues. The sample slides on this page are from a presentation called "Animal Rights and Wrongs." The slides on the opposite page are from her "Vegetarian is the New Prius" talk.

"When dealing with a complex or controversial issue, it is important to communicate your ideas in a way that the audience can relate to and visualize," Sangeeta says. "In these examples, rather than relying on bar graphs or heady quotes, I use engaging photographs and easy-to-understand facts to help the audience visualize how their food choices impact animals and the environment."

See more designs by Sangeeta on her corporate website:

www.kumaridesigns.com

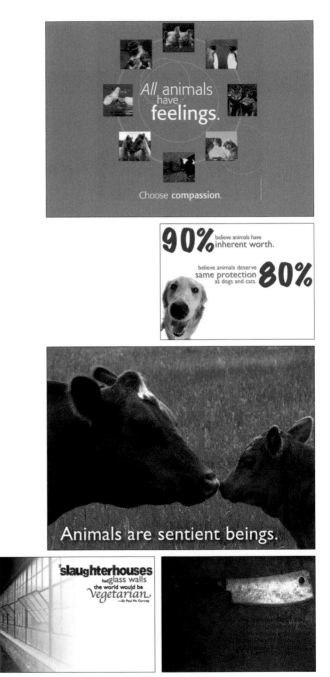

Saturated fat and cholesterol is #1 cause of heart disease

Heart Disease #1 killer in US

Vegetarian Is The New Prius | Meat Eating and the Environment

"...one of the most significant contributors to today's most serious environmental problems."

UN Food and Agricultural Organization | Meat Eating and the Environment

70% of forest in Amazon is used for cattle grazing

Rain Forest Destruction | Primary Cause: Cattle-grazing

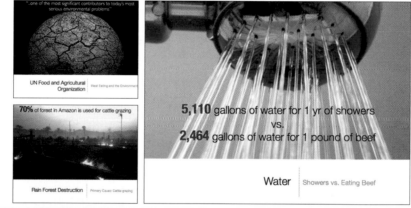

5,110 gallons of water for 1 yr of showers
vs.
2,464 gallons of water for 1 pound of beef

Water | Showers vs. Eating Beef

a vegetarian spares **100** animals per year

Resources | sangeetak@peta.org

Veg 101 | A guide to a healthier YOU

Doctor Impresses Crowd at Medical Symposium

Andreas Eenfeldt is a young, 6'8" medical doctor from Sweden who is very interested in presenting differently. I first met Andreas at one of my Presentation Zen seminars in Paris. He is a good example of someone doing important work and making an impact, using his knowledge and experience to challenge conventional wisdom and create a dramatic change. "It's time for a health revolution," he says. To create this revolution, he realized early on that engaging presentation skills were necessary to spread the word. Recently, Andreas gave an impressive presentation at the Ancestral Health Symposium 2011.

I liked Andreas's AHS 2011 presentation, which got a lot of attention, for many reasons. The presentation had a good flow and structure that provided enough evidence to support his statements. He provided personal stories of his friends balanced with data and quotations from credible people in the field that supported his idea. He also told personal stories. Andreas was not always such an engaging presenter, so I asked him about his transformation:

> "Fall-asleep-boring presentations are no exceptions in the medical field—they are the norm. This is good news, of course, because even small improvements are all that's needed for presentations to stand out today. Back in 2008, I had started to do more and more presentations on low carb nutrition. It was then pointed out to me that just reading to the audience from my slides was not optimal. My presentation skills back then (just three years ago) were as bad or worse than your average MD's. I started Googling and watching some YouTube videos on the subject. Pretty soon I ended up on the Presentation Zen website and have probably read every post on the site and read all of the Presentation Zen books and Nancy Duarte's books and most of the books recommended on presentationzen.com. I have also lectured about 150 times in Swedish since then, and four times in English. So, in just three years my presentation skills improved from awful to pretty decent (even in my second language). Makes me wonder what my talks are going to be like 10 years from now."

For preparation, Andreas says he brainstormed using sticky notes on his whiteboard, and then filtered out the most important points, arranging them into groups, creating messages, and organizing them in the best order. The opposite page shows a few of his more than 100 slides used in the 45-minute presentation.

These two visuals are from early in his presentation—the exposition stage—where he introduces the problem. That is, that the obesity epidemic is a recent phenomenon.

The doctor then used statistical evidence from the CDC over 14 slides (four of which are shown here) featuring a map of the United States that changes to reflect in a clear and visceral way the dramatic increase in obesity over a 27-year period.

"**Two generations of Swedes have been given** bad dietary advice and have avoided fat for no reason. **It's time to rewrite the dietary guidelines and base them on modern science.**"

Göran Berglund
Professor of Internal Medicine, Lund

Interview in *The Daily News*, Sweden's biggest newspaper. December 2009.

"**It's time to face the facts. There is no connection between saturated fats and cardiovascular disease.**"

Peter Nilsson
Professor of Cardiovascular Research, Lund

Lecture in front of 500 Swedish doctors. January, 2010.

A useful presentation technique is to use quotes from credible sources to support your assertions. Andreas displayed quotes a few times in this talk—in large type with key phrases highlighted, producing a very simple and clear design that was easily seen from the back of the hall.

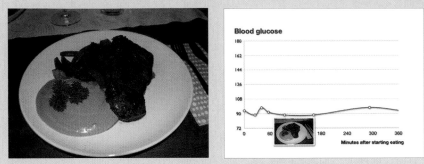

The doctor shares a personal example, shown here. After a home-cooked LCHF (low carbohydrate high fat) meal in Sweden, he tested his blood glucose, which remained rather stable as shown clearly in the simple chart.

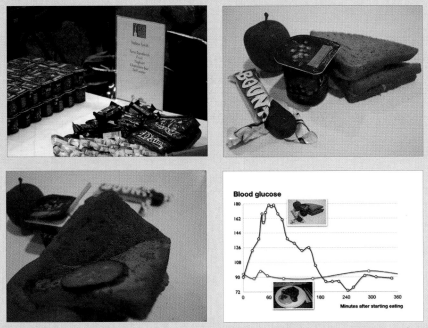

Then, Andreas went on to compare his LCHF meal to a high carb lunch with loads of sugars that he was served—ironically enough—at an obesity conference in Stockholm. While this example is just his personal experience, it very much resonated with the audience. A very simple, clear, and visual explanation.

My Declaration
of Independence

Real freedom begins at home

My Declaration of Independence

Pam Slim
Speaker, Coach, Business Consultant
www.escapefromcubiclenation.com

The few slides shown here are from a longer presentation called "My Declaration of Independence." Pam Slim and her team designed these slides for use in both live presentations and an inspirational piece done in Flash and set to music that is on her website. For the live talk, Pam can remove more of the text so the slides complement her words.

You can watch the Flash version of this presentation on Pam's corporate site, Ganas Consulting:

www.ganas.com

Takahashi Method

Masayoshi Takahashi

Web Application Developer, Tokyo, Japan

www.rubycolor.org/takahashi/

www.slideshare.net/takahashim

Masayoshi Takahashi is a programmer who created a new approach to presenting at tech conferences in Japan. Takahashi uses only text in his slides. But not just any text—really big text. Huge text. Characters of impressive proportion which rarely number more than a few per slide. The goal, he says, is to use short words rather than long, complicated words and phrases. His approach—now called the Takahashi Method—came about several years ago when he had to give a short presentation at a conference in Japan. He did not have software like PowerPoint, he says, nor did he have access to photos or drawing programs. He was stuck with text (projected in a Web browser). So he started thinking very hard about how to use the best word for each slide as he took the audience through his presentation. The words or phrases resemble Japanese newspaper headlines rather than sentences that must be read. His slides, though they are all text, are visual in the sense that (if you read Japanese) they are instantly understood and support his talk. As he says, if you have bullets or sentences, the audience will read those and may miss what you are saying.

While it may not be a perfect method or applicable in all situations, it is still far better than the method used by many conference presenters in Japan (dull, bulleted talking points projected on a screen). The slides Takahashi uses in his presentations are displayed at a rapid pace and number well over a hundred per talk. The samples here are just a few from a live presentation where he explained the origins of his "Takahashi Method." Check out his Slideshare link above to see more samples.

高橋
メソッド

プレゼン
テーションの
一手法

特徴

巨大な
文字

簡潔な
言葉

Inbox Zero

Merlin Mann
Productivity Guru and Creator of 43 folders

www.43folders.com
www.merlinmann.com

The slides shown here are part of a talk Merlin Mann gave in the summer of 2007 at Google's Tech Talk series. The presentation was about strategies for dealing with high-volume e-mail and the importance of getting your inbox to zero. These simple slides—created with images from iStockphoto.com—served as a good supportive backdrop for his story. You can find a video of Merlin's "Inbox Zero" presentation on YouTube.

In Sum

A good visual enhances the speaker's message. The sample slides featured here highlight what's possible when you combine images and text. From a technical point of view, these slides were not too difficult to produce. All the designer needed was PowerPoint or Keynote along with image editing software such as Adobe Photoshop Elements. What you design your slides or other visuals to look like depends completely on your unique situation, content, and audience, but keep the following in mind:

- Create visuals that are simple and feature clear design priorities and elements that guide the viewer's eye.

- Use a visual theme, but avoid tired, overused software templates.

- Limit bullet points or avoid them completely.

- Use high-quality graphics.

- Build (animate) complex graphics to support your narrative.

- Think "maximum effect with minimum means."

- Learn to see empty space, and learn to use it in a way that brings greater clarity to visuals.

delivery

Be here now. Be someplace else later.
Is that so complicated?

— David Bader

The Art of Being Completely Present

8

We are offended when we try to have a conversation or a meeting with someone who seems preoccupied—someone who is not fully "there," listening and contributing. Yet we have become quite accustomed to enduring speakers and presenters who are not fully engaged with the audience and the topic. One of the most important things to remember when delivering a presentation is to be fully present at that moment. A good presenter is fully committed to the moment, committed to being there with the audience at that particular place and time. He may have pressing problems—who doesn't?—but he puts those aside so that he may be fully there. When you give a presentation, your mind should not be racing with a million concerns, distracted from the here and now. It is impossible to have a real conversation with someone when he is "somewhere else." Likewise, it is impossible to give a truly successful presentation when you are "somewhere else."

One of the most fundamental things you can learn from the world of Zen is the art of mindfulness. You may know of mindfulness in its association with meditation (*zazen*). But the interesting thing about Zen is that it is not separate from the real world. That is, Zen makes no distinction between ordinary life and spiritual life. Meditation is not an escape from reality at all; in fact, even everyday routines can be methods for meditation. When you are aware that your actions and judgments are usually just automatic reactions based on a sort of running dialogue in your head, then you are free to let go of such judgments. So, rather than hating washing the dishes, you just wash the dishes. When you write a letter, you write a letter. And when you give a presentation, you give a presentation.

Mindfulness is concerned with the here and now—with having an awareness of this particular moment. You want to see this moment as it is without your ordinary filters, filters that are concerned only with the past (or future) and how things should or will be and so on. True mindfulness is accessible to all, although it is not easy to obtain. Our lives are so crazy these days with answering e-mail, sending text messages, surfing the Web, or driving late in rush hour traffic to pick up the kids while ordering dinner on a mobile phone. There are so many things on our minds and so many worries. Worries are the worst things of all because they are always about the past or about the future—two things that do not even exist in the present. In our daily lives and in our work lives, including giving presentations, we've got to clear our minds and be in only one place: right here.

(Photo: Justin Sullivan/iStockphoto.com.)

Steve Jobs and the Art of the Swordsman

As noted in Chapter 5, Steve Jobs had a simple yet remarkable approach to the art of presentation. His slides, for example, were always devoid of clutter and highly visual, and he used them smoothly and seamlessly, advancing all slides and effects by himself without ever drawing attention to the fact that he was the one advancing the slides. His style was conversational, and his visuals were in perfect sync with his words. His presentations were built on a solid structure, which gave them an easy feeling of flow as if he were taking us on a small journey. On stage he seemed friendly, comfortable, and confident (which make others feel relaxed too), and he exuded a level of passion and enthusiasm that was engaging without being over the top.

It all seemed so automatic and natural. It all seemed so easy that you'd be tempted to think it just came naturally to Steve, and that it was a pretty easy task for him to use his natural charisma to woo a crowd. But you'd be wrong. While it is true that Steve Jobs was a charismatic figure, I'm not sure giving presentations with multimedia support, and even giving live demos (how many executives do that?), comes naturally to anyone. No, the reason Steve Jobs's presentations went so well and were so engaging was because he and his team prepared and practiced like mad to make sure it looked "easy."

When Steve was on stage he was an artist. And like any artist, through practice and experience, he perfected his technique and form. Yet, also like a trained artist, there was no thought of technique or of form, or even of failure or success while performing the art of presentation. Once we think of failure or success, we are like the swordsman whose mind stops, ever so briefly, to ponder his technique or the outcome of the fight. The moment he does, he has lost. This sounds paradoxical, but once we allow our minds to drift to thoughts of success and failure or of outcomes and technique while performing our art, we have at that moment begun our descent. Steve Jobs's approach to presentation reminds us today that engagement can be enhanced by being nowhere else but completely here in the moment.

To see videos of presentations by Steve Jobs, go to the Apple website: *www.apple.com/apple-events*

The Mind That Is No Mind

When a swordsman is in the moment and his mind is empty (*mushin no shin* or the "mind that is no mind"), there are no emotions stemming from fear and no thoughts of winning, losing, or even using the sword. In this way, says Daisetz T. Suzuki in *Zen and Japanese Culture* (Princeton University Press), "both man and sword turn into instruments in the hands of the unconscious, and it is the unconscious that achieves wonders of creativity. It is here that swordplay becomes an art."

Beyond mastering technique, the secret to swordsmanship rests in obtaining a proper mental state of "no mind" where the mind is "abandoned and yet not abandoned." Frankly, if you are engaged in any art or even a sports match, you must get rid of the obtruding self-consciousness or ego-consciousness and apply yourself completely. As Suzuki says, it must be "as if nothing particular were taking place at the moment." When you perform in a state of "no mind," you are free from the burdens of inhibitions and doubt and can contribute fully and fluidly in the moment. Artists know this state of mind, as do musicians and highly trained athletes.

The highly anticipated presentations that Steve Jobs did came with a lot of pressure to get it right. A lot was riding on each presentation and expectations were high inside and outside of Apple. Yet what made Steve so effective in these situations was his ability to seemingly forget the seriousness of the situation and just perform. In this way, he was like the artful swordsman who, through his "immovable mind," has no thought of life or death. The mind has been quieted, and the man is free to be fully present. As Suzuki puts it: "The waters are in motion all the time, but the moon retains its serenity. The mind moves in response to ten thousand situations but remains ever the same."

Technical training is important, but technical training is something acquired and will always have the feel of artificiality unless one has the proper state of mind. "Unless the mind which avails itself of the technical skill somehow attunes itself to a state of the utmost fluidity or mobility," says Suzuki, "anything acquired or superimposed lacks spontaneity of natural growth." In this sense, I think instructors and books can help us become better at presenting, but ultimately, like many other performance arts, it must grow within us.

You need technique and proper form, and you need to know "the rules." You must practice and then practice some more. When you put in the hard work in the preparation phase and internalize the material, you can perform the art of presentation in a way that is more natural by obtaining the proper state of mind—that is, "no mind."

Lost in the Moment

Have you ever been lost in the moment while presenting or performing? I do not mean lost as in losing your place. I mean being so in the moment—without worry of the past or future—that you are as demonstrably interested in your topic as your audience has become. This is a true connection.

In *If You Want to Write*, Brenda Ueland speaks of the importance of being in the moment to maximize your creativity and impact on an audience. Harnessing this creative energy and being fully present is more of an intuitive activity, not an intellectual one. Brenda compares this kind of creativity and connection to a wonderful musical performance.

In playing a musical instrument such as a piano, for example, sometimes you play at it and sometimes you play in it. The goal is not to repeat the notes on the page, but to play beautiful music. To be *in it*, not separate from it. Great musicians play in it (even if they are not always technically perfect). The same thing holds for presentations. The aim should be to be in it completely at that moment in time. Perfect technique is perhaps not obtainable (or even desirable), but a kind of perfect connection can exist between the audience and artist (or presenter) when she "plays in it."

"Only when you play in a thing," Brenda says, "do people listen and hear you and are moved." Your music is believable and authentic because you are "lost in it," not intellectualizing it or following a set of prescribed rules (notes, instructions). We are moved because the artist is clearly and authentically moved as well. Can this not hold true for presentations? Your presentation is believable because you are prepared and logical, but also because you too are moved by your topic. You have to believe in your message completely or no one else will. You must believe in your story fully and be "lost in the moment" of engaging your audience.

"The waters are in motion all the time, but the moon retains its serenity. The mind moves in response to ten thousand situations but remains ever the same."

—Daisetz T. Suzuki

Learning from the Art of Judo

You can find the best presentation advice in unusual places. Consider the following five principles, for example. These precepts offer good advice for delivering effective presentations:

1. Carefully observe oneself and one's situation, carefully observe others, and carefully observe one's environment.
2. Seize the initiative in whatever you undertake.
3. Consider fully, act decisively.
4. Know when to stop.
5. Keep to the middle.

These are wise words indeed, but they are not actually "effective presentation principles." They are Jigoro Kano's Five Principles of Judo as outlined by John Stevens in *Budo Secrets* (Shambhala, New Ed edition). Yet, it is easy to see how these principles can be applied in your efforts to design and deliver presentations. For example, you may have witnessed a presentation in which the speaker could have done much better if he had only embraced the wisdom of principle No. 4—know when to stop. At times, you may speak for a longer or shorter time than planned, but it must be a conscious decision based on the context of the moment and by following principle No. 1—observing oneself, the situation, others, and the environment. These are just two examples illustrating the application of such principles.

Jigoro Kano founded judo in the late 1800s in Japan. While it is not based on the principles of Zen outright, judo is seen by many to be a great expression of Zen concepts. I have a mountain of respect for people who dedicate themselves to the art of judo. Judo is more than a sport or mere physical activity. To those who practice it, the lessons, wisdom, and experience gained serve to help them in profound ways in all aspects of life.

Commenting on the secrets of judo, H. Seichiro Okazaki said: "Only by cultivating a receptive state of mind, without preconceived ideas or thoughts, can one master the secret art of reacting spontaneously and naturally without hesitation and without purposeless resistance." This idea need not be confined to the judo mat. Think about the last challenging presentation you made that did not go as well as you had hoped. Perhaps there was more "pushback" than you expected. Could you have done better by engaging your audience and answering the difficult questions while "reacting spontaneously and naturally without hesitation and without purposeless resistance?" In my experience, when I have received challenging questions from a skeptical or even hostile or aggressive person, a natural, nonaggressive response from myself always proves more effective than showing irritation or defensiveness. Butting heads is very easy to do, but it usually leads to a sure defeat for the presenter.

Presenting Under Fire

At some point, you will encounter a hostile client or an audience member who may be more interested in making you look foolish or derailing your talk than getting at the truth. It happens. The key is to remember that they are never the enemy. If there is an enemy at all, it is within us. Even if an audience member does choose to assume the role of "opponent," your irritation or display of anger will surely not do you or the rest of your audience—90 percent of whom may support your views—any good.

In the world of judo, founder Jigoro Kano had this to say about dealing with an opponent: "Victory over the opponent is achieved by giving way to the strength of the opponent, adapting to it and taking advantage of it, turning it in the end to your own advantage."

Many years ago I was giving a presentation to a large group. It was going very well, but one person in the audience often interrupted with irrelevant comments to the point of becoming a distraction for the audience. I had many occasions to become angry, but did not. I could sense that the audience believed I was going to rip into the guy if there was one more interruption. And frankly, they would not have blamed me. But I remained respectful of the man and did not show any irritation or anger, nor did I allow his interruptions to derail the talk. After the presentation, several people complimented me on my handling of the "interrupter." The ironic thing was that while the boisterous man may have intended to damage my effectiveness, he actually had the opposite influence. By flowing with the moment, showing self-control, and not butting heads with him—which only would have made things worse—I gained respect from the audience.

Contribution and Being in the Moment

Every presentation is a performance, and Ben Zander knows a thing or two about the art of performance. You may know Ben Zander as the talented conductor for the Boston Philharmonic Orchestra, but he is also one of the truly gifted presenters of our time. He's so good, in fact, so inspiring and so informative, that he could spend all his time just talking to companies and organizations about leadership and transformation.

As Dan Pink and I were riding the train back to central Osaka in the spring of 2007, he tipped me off to Ben Zander. There are a lot of good presenters, Dan said, but Ben Zander is in another league. That same day, I purchased *The Art of Possibility: Transforming Professional and Personal Life* (Penguin) by Rosamund and Benjamin Zander, and I was inspired. Dan's suggestion to check out Ben Zander as a speaker/presenter was the best tip I had received in a long time. Ironically, the next month I presented for a Fortune 500 company and found that every single person in the room was well-versed in Zanders's teachings and their simple advice had a powerful effect within the company.

Here's a sample of the kind of remarkable messages Ben conveys to his audiences. In this case, he is talking about musicianship, but his words can be applied to most of our presentation situations, too:

> *"This is the moment—this is the most important moment right now. Which is: We are about contribution. That's what our job is. It's not about impressing people. It's not about getting the next job. It's about contributing something."*
>
> — *Benjamin Zander*

It's not always about success or failure, it's about contribution and being fully present. Rather than asking questions such as "Will I be appreciated?" or "Will I win them over?" and so on, ask "How can I make a contribution?" Here is what Ben said to a talented young musician while coaching him on his musical performance: "We are about contribution, that's what our job is... everyone was clear you contributed passion to the people in this room. Did you do it better than the next violinist, or did he do better than a pianist? I don't care, because in contribution, there is no better!"

The Zanders say that rather than getting bogged down in a sea of measurement—during which you compare yourself to others and worry about whether you are worthy to be making the presentation or whether someone else could be doing it better—instead realize that at this moment, right here right now, you are the gift. Your message is the contribution. There is no "better," there is only now. It really is pretty simple.

Not every presentation situation is about contribution, perhaps, but most are. In fact, I don't think I have ever given a presentation that was not at some level about making a contribution. Certainly, when you are asked to share your expertise with a group of people who are, on the whole, not specialists in your field, you have to think very hard about what is important (for them) and what is not (again, *for them*). It is easier just to do the same presentation you always do, but it is not about impressing people with the depths of your knowledge. It's about sharing or teaching something of lasting value.

Passion, Risk, and "Playing on One Buttock"

In most cultures—and certainly in Japan—making a mistake is the worst thing you can do. Ben Zander says it's dangerous for musicians, for example, to be so concerned with competition and measuring themselves against others because this makes it "difficult to take the necessary risks with themselves to become great performers." Only through mistakes can you see where you're lacking, where you need to work. We hate mistakes, so we play it safe. Yet long term, nothing could be more dangerous if your goal is to be great at what you do. Zander suggests that instead of getting so dejected by mistakes, we instead exclaim loudly, raise our arms, and shout "How fascinating!" every time we make a mistake. Think about that. Another mistake? How fascinating! Another opportunity to learn something just presented itself. Another unlucky break? No worries! Move forward. You cannot worry about mistakes and be fully present in the moment at the same time.

It is not enough to know a piece of music intellectually or to play it without any mistakes—you have to convey the true language of the music emotionally, says Ben. When musicians truly got into the music and play it with such heart and emotion that audiences were moved beyond words, Ben noticed that the music flowed through the musicians, taking control of their bodies as they swayed from side to side. Zander, then, urges musicians to become "one-buttock players," that is to let the music flow through their bodies, causing them to lean and to move from one buttock to the other. If you're a musician, or you're making a performance of virtually any kind, and you are totally in the moment and connecting with the language of the music and the audience, there is no way you can be a "two-buttock player." You've got to move, you've got to connect, and you must not hold back your passion. Instead, you must let the audience have a taste of the commitment, energy, and passion you have for the music (or the topic, the ideas, etc.).

You can hold back, aim not to make an error, and play it perfectly "on two buttocks." Or, you can say, "Screw it!—I'll take a risk," and dare to lean into the music with intensity, color, humanity, and passion and quite possibly, in your own small way (and on only one buttock), change the world. Play it with total sincerity and with your entire body—heart and soul—and you will make a connection and change things. As Ben Zander said while encouraging one of his talented students to play it in the "one-buttock" style: "If you play that way, they won't be able to resist you. You will be a compelling force behind which everyone will be inspired to play their best."

Jazz pianist Dr. John Hanagan is fully in the moment while playing in a popular jazz club in Osaka, Japan. That's me on drums and "Taku" is playing bass off camera. (Photo: Nikolas Papageorgiou.)

Don't Take Yourself So Seriously!

"Lighten up," says Ben Zander, "and you lighten up those around you." This is not to suggest that you shouldn't take your work seriously (you should), or even that you shouldn't take yourself seriously (that may depend on the time and place), but as an absolute certainty, we must all get over ourselves. There is perhaps no better way to get over ourselves than the use of humor.

Rosamund Zander, the philosopher of the partnership, says that from birth we are concerned about measurement and worried about the perceived scarcity of love, attention, food, and so on that seems to be the way of the world. She calls this the "calculating self," and in this environment of scarcity, competition, and comparison, "the self needs to be taken very seriously indeed." No matter how successful and confident you may become as an adult, your "calculating self" (concerned with measurement and worried about scarcity) is weak and sees itself at risk of losing everything.

The goal, then, is to move away from the calculating self, the self that lives in a world of scarcity, exaggerated threats, and deficiencies, and move toward a healthier attitude of sufficiency, wholeness, and possibilities. Getting over yourself—humor is a great vehicle for this—allows you to see the "creative nature of the world and ourselves." When you understand what an infant can't—that is, you cannot control the world, you cannot impose your will on people's hearts—you begin to get over yourself.

When you learn to lighten up, you see yourself as permeable, not vulnerable, says Rosamund, and you stay open to the unknown, new influences, and new ideas. Rather than trying to resist and fight the river of life, you move through it with a harmonious fluidity and grace, learning to join rather than resist the flow. Humor is a wonderful way to remind everyone around us—no matter how hard the work gets—that our true and most "central" self is not obsessed with childish demands, entitlements, and calculations but is instead supportive, confident, helpful, and even inspiring. A presentation is as good a time as any to let people see that side of you.

In Sum

- Like a conversation, presentation requires your full presence at that time and place.

- Like a master swordsman, you must be completely in the moment without thoughts of the past, the future, winning, or losing.

- Mistakes may happen, but do not dwell on past mistakes or worry about future ones. Be only in this moment, sharing and conversing with the audience in front of you.

- You will make it look easy and natural by preparing and practicing like mad. The more you rehearse, the more confident you'll become, and the easier it will seem to the audience.

- Although you must plan well, being fully in the moment also means that you remain flexible, totally aware, and open to the possibilities as they arise.

9

Connecting with an Audience

Most of what I have learned about communication and connection did not come from my speech and communication classes in school. It came from my experience as a performer and from years of closely watching others perform. I worked my way through college playing drums in various jazz groups beginning when I was 17. No matter how technically "good" the music was, I have never seen a great performance that lacked a solid connection between the performer and the audience.

Playing music is a performance and also very much a presentation. Good presentations are about conversing, sharing, and connecting on an intellectual *and* emotional level in an honest and sincere way. It is even easier to connect when playing music since everything is right out there for everyone to see and hear. It doesn't get much more honest than jazz, which has been called "the music of dialogue." There are no politics and no walls. The music may touch the audience or it may not, but there is never even a hint of insincerity, questionable motives, or pretense of being anything other than what people see before them at that moment. The smiles, the heads nodding in agreement, and the feet tapping under the tables tell me that there is a connection, and that connection is no less than communication. It's a fantastic feeling.

Tom Grant, based in Portland, Oregon, is a musical legend in America's Pacific Northwest. You can buy his albums and hear his songs on jazz and soft jazz stations around the world, including in Japan. Tom is a great musician, but what I always like about his live performances is his warmth and friendly, engaging style that just make the connection with the audience so much better.

The lesson I've learned from watching great live musical performances is that the music plus the artist's ability to convey the (musical) message and connect with the audience is what it's all about. If done well, the end result is far more than just the notes played. A true performance transcends the simple act of artists playing music and people listening. It's bigger than that.

The art of musical performance and the art of presentation share the same essence. That is, it's always about bridging the distance between the artist and audience to make a real connection. If there's no connection, there can be no conversation. This is true whether you're pitching a new technology, explaining a new medical treatment, or playing at Carnegie Hall.

To Tom Grant, performance is not an exhibition—I perform, you listen. Tom clearly feels it's a two-way encounter. Here's what Tom said in an interview in *Smooth Vibes* in 2005: "There is joy in music for the player and for the receiver. I play music because it is my calling in life. I hope it conveys a joy and benevolence that people can apply to their own lives and thus improve, if only in the tiniest way, the quality of life on earth."

Photo of Tom Grant by Owen Carey.

Are not presentations about the player (presenter) and the receiver (audience)? A good tip to always remember: It's not about us, it's about them. And about the message.

Jazz, Zen, and the Art of Connection

There is a line of thinking that says if I tell you the meaning of Zen, then it wouldn't really be Zen. The same could be said concerning the meaning of jazz. Of course, we can talk about them and label them. With our verbalization, we get close to the meanings—and the discussion may be interesting, helpful, and even inspiring. Yet we never experience the thing itself by talking about it. Zen is concerned with the thing itself. Zen is about the now—right here, right now. The essence of jazz expression is like this, too. It's about this moment. No artificiality, no pretending to be anything you're not. No acting. No wishing at this moment to be anywhere or with anyone except where you are.

While there are many forms of jazz, if you want to at least get close to the essence of the art, then listen to the 1959 album *Kind of Blue* by Miles Davis. The liner notes for this classic album were written by the legendary Bill Evans, who plays piano on the recording. In these notes, Bill makes a direct reference to one of the Zen arts, *sumi-e*. Here are just a few lines from his notes:

"There is a Japanese visual art in which the artist is forced to be spontaneous. He must paint on a thin stretched parchment with a special brush and black water paint in such a way that an unnatural or interrupted stroke will destroy the line or break through the parchment. Erasures or changes are impossible. These artists must practice a particular discipline, that of allowing the idea to express itself in communication with their hands in such a direct way that deliberation cannot interfere."

I always thought there was a sort of aesthetic to this album that expressed the tenets of restraint, simplicity, and naturalness—principles that are at the heart of the Presentation Zen approach as well. In the music you hear a free yet structured spontaneity, an idea that seems oxymoronic until you study one of the Zen arts—or jazz. A free yet structured spontaneity is exactly the kind of state we want to be in with an audience during a presentation.

You can establish better connections with an audience by bringing the spirit of jazz to your talk. By "spirit of jazz," I mean the complete opposite of how people usually use the term *jazz*—as in "jazz it up," that is, decorate it or add something on the surface. The spirit of jazz is about honest intention. If the intent is pure and the message clear, then that is all you can do. Jazz means removing the barriers and making it accessible, helping people to get your expression (your message, story, point). This does not necessarily mean you will always be direct, although this is often the clearest path. Hint and suggestion are powerful, too. The difference is that hint and suggestion with intent have a purpose and are done with the audience in mind. Hint and suggestion without intent or sincerity may result in simplistic, ineffective ramblings or even obfuscation.

Jazz makes the complex simple through profound expressions of clarity and sincerity. It has structure and rules but also great freedom. Above all, jazz is natural. It is not about putting on a façade of sophistication or seriousness. In fact, humor and playfulness are also at the core of jazz. You may be a dedicated, serious musician or you may be an appreciative fan, but either way you also understand that to be human is to laugh and to play—play is natural to us and natural to the creative process. It's only through our formal education that we begin to doubt the "seriousness" of play. When this happens, we begin to lose a bit of ourselves, including our confidence and a bit of our humanity. I've found through my parallel studies of jazz and the Zen arts that both have structure and practice at their core along with a strong component of playfulness and laughter—all elements we would like to bring to our presentations as well.

Quotes from Jazz

Jazz is about dialogue. It's about making connections and being fully in the moment. When discussing this point in live presentations, I often introduce quotes by famous musicians. The four quotes on the slides here speak to the art of presentation and making connections as well. (Embedded slide images from iStockphoto.com.)

> "If they act too hip, you know they can't play s**t!"
>
> — Louis Armstrong

With practice we can become more polished. But too much polish turns a presentation into a TV-like infomercial unworthy of an audience's trust. Presentation is a very human thing. Practice, rehearse, and make it great. But keep it real. Keep it human. And remember that it is about them (the audience), not us.

> "Master your instrument. Master the music. And then forget all that bulls**t and just play."
>
> — Charlie-Parker

Studying design, presentation, and communication is crucial. Obviously, you must know your subject well. But when we present, all that matters is that moment and that audience. Get to the point. Tell them something memorable. Quit worrying and inspire them or teach them—or better yet, both.

IT'S TAKEN ME ALL MY LIFE
TO LEARN WHAT NOT TO PLAY.

DIZZY-GILLESPIE

Most presentations are too long or filled with unnecessary information that is included for the wrong reasons (such as fear). Knowing what to leave out takes work. Again, anyone can include everything and say everything. It is the master presenters (or writers, artists, and so on) who know what to exclude and have the courage to cut it.

"You can play a shoestring if you're sincere."

—John Coltrane

In most situations, you don't need the latest technology or the best equipment in the world. Showing that you are well prepared and ready to present naked, with or without technology, is far more important. A poor presentation is not any better simply because expensive equipment is used to project images. Sincerity, honesty, and respect for the audience matter far more than technology and technique.

Start Strong to Make a Connection

To establish a connection with an audience, we must grab their attention right from the start. Granville N. Toogood, author of *The Articulate Executive,* also emphasizes starting off quickly and beginning with punch. "To make sure you don't get off on the wrong foot, plunge right in," he says. "To galvanize the mind of the audience, you've got to strike quickly." I always urge people not to waste time at the beginning of a presentation with formalities such as long introductions or filler talk that is not related to the presentation's goal. The beginning is the most important part. You need an opening that grabs people and brings them in. If you fail to hook them at the start, the rest of your presentation may be for naught.

The primacy effect in the context of presentations suggests that we remember more strongly what happens at the beginning of a presentation. There are many ways to strike quickly and start with punch to make a strong initial connection. In my book *The Naked Presenter* (New Riders), I introduced the idea of making a strong connection by incorporating into your opening content that which is personal, unexpected, novel, challenging, or humorous. Not coincidentally, these elements comprise the acronym PUNCH to help you remember. Most of the best presentations contain at least one or more of these elements. Let's take a look at PUNCH in more detail.

PERSONAL

Make it personal. Personal in this case does not mean a long self-introduction about your background complete with organizational charts or why you are qualified to speak. A personal and relevant story, however, can be a very effective opening so long as it illustrates a key engaging point or sets the theme in a memorable way.

UNEXPECTED

Reveal something unexpected. Doing something or saying something that goes against what people expect gets their attention. Do or say something that taps into the emotion of surprise. This emotion increases alertness and gets people to focus. "There must be surprise…some key facts that are not commonly known or are counterintuitive," says management guru Tom Peters. "No reason to do the presentation in the first place if there are no surprises."

NOVEL

Show or tell something novel. Get people's attention by introducing something new. Start with a powerful image that's never been seen, reveal a relevant short story that's never been heard, or show a statistic from a brand-new study that gives new insights into a problem. Chances are your audience is filled with natural born explorers who crave discovery and are attracted to the new and the unknown. Novelty is threatening for some people, but assuming the environment is safe and there is not an over abundance of novelty in the environment, your audience will be seeking the novel and new.

CHALLENGING

Challenge conventional wisdom or challenge the audience's assumptions. Consider challenging people's imaginations, too: "How would you like to fly from New York to Tokyo in two hours? Impossible? Well, some experts think it's possible!" Challenge people intellectually by asking provocative questions that make them think. Many presentations and lectures fail because they simply attempt to transfer information from speaker to listener as if the listeners were not active participants.

HUMOROUS

Use humor to connect with the audience through a shared laugh. There are many benefits to laughter. Laughter is contagious. An audience that shares a laugh becomes more connected with each other and with you, creating a positive vibe in the room. Laughter releases endorphins, relaxes the whole body, and can even change one's perspective. The old adage is if they are laughing, they are listening. This is true, although it does not necessarily mean they are learning. It is critical, however, that the humor be directly relevant to the topic at hand or otherwise fit harmoniously into the flow of the narrative without distracting you from the objective of your talk.

The concept of recommending humor in a presentation gets a bad rap because of the common and tired practice of opening up a speech with a joke, almost always a lame one. However, I'm not talking about telling jokes. Forget about jokes. On the other hand, an observation of irony, an anecdote, or a short humorous story that makes a relevant point or introduces the topic and sets the theme are the kinds of openings that can work.

There are many ways to start a presentation, but no matter how you choose to start, do not waste those initial valuable two or three minutes "warming up" the audience with filler material or formalities. Start strong. The five elements comprising PUNCH are not the only options to consider, but if your opening contains at least one of these approaches, then you are on your way to opening with impact and making a strong connection.

The Honeymoon Period

Getting and keeping an audience's attention can be a tricky thing. Generally, audience's want you to succeed, but they will still only give you one or two minutes of a "honeymoon period" for you to make a good impression. Even famous, well-established presenters, including celebrities, will only get about a minute before audiences grow tired of a presenter's inability to make a good impression and grab their attention. There is no excuse for a weak start. If your technology lets you down just as your presentation starts, you cannot stop. As they say in show business: "The show must go on." People form impressions of you and the presentation in the first few moments. You never want those first few moments to be a memory of you trying to get the technology to work.

Never Start with an Apology

Do not apologize or imply that you have not prepared enough for a given audience. It may be true, and your apology may be sincere and honest (rather than just being an excuse), but it never comes across well to an audience. The audience does not need to know that we have not prepared as much as we would have liked, so why mention it and get it in their head? You actually may be prepared enough and doing well, but now the audiences is saying to themselves "Man, he's right—he didn't prepare enough." The same goes for telling people you're nervous. "You didn't look nervous, but now that you mention it…."

A confession that you are nervous may seem honest and transparent, but it is too self-focused at a time when you are supposed to be focused on the audience and their needs and their feelings. An admission about being nervous is not said to make the audience feel better, only to make yourself feel better. If you admit that you are nervous, you may actually feel better since labeling and acknowledging your emotion is better than suppressing it. This is why people say it—because saying it out loud does make you feel a little better. However, the presentation is about the audience, and telling them how nervous you are does not serve their interest. Acknowledge to yourself that you are nervous. Being nervous is normal and saying it to yourself will help you feel better. But you do not need to share this information with the audience.

Do You Need to Show the Structure?

Do not start with an agenda slide. After you have made an initial connection with the audience, however, it's a good idea to give people an idea of where you are going during your time. Usually you can do this verbally in just a few seconds. But, if you have a lot of material, you may want to show the audience how your talk is structured and then remind them along the way where you are in the presentation. In a 2007 Macworld keynote presentation, Steve Jobs did this by breaking his presentation into three "Acts" and displaying the number of the act before each of his three sections.

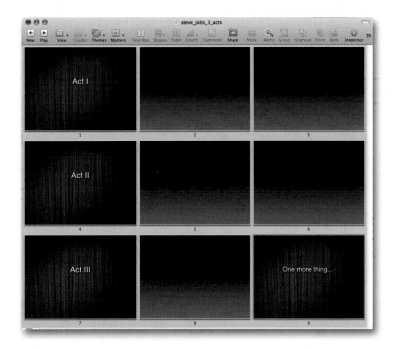

Project Yourself

To make a connection you cannot be timid—you must project yourself. There are three things to consider when evaluating your ability to project yourself to an audience aside from the content of the talk: The way you look, the way you move, and the way you sound. The audience members, whether they know it or not, are judging you and your message based on these elements. All these factors influence your ability to make a strong connection.

Look the Part

How you dress matters. A rule of thumb is to dress at least a little more formally than your audience. It's important to dress appropriate to the organization and the occasion, of course, but it's better to be a bit overdressed than underdressed. You want to project an image of professionalism, but you do not want to seem out of touch with your audience either. In Silicon Valley, for example, the dress code can be quite casual and even a well-groomed person in jeans with a quality shirt and a good pair of shoes may look professional. (When we occasionally saw people in business suits on the Apple campus, we could tell they were from out of town.) In Tokyo, both men and women cannot go wrong with a dark business suit virtually anywhere. You can always bring your formality down a notch by removing your jacket, removing the tie, and rolling up the sleeves, but it's difficult to dress up a look that is too casual. To be safe, and to show respect for your audience, err on the side of dressing up.

Move with Purpose

If you can avoid it, do not stand in one place during the entire presentation. It's far better to walk to different parts of the stage or room, which allows you to engage with more people. You should not, however, pace back and forth or wander around the area near the screen without purpose. This kind of movement is distracting and projects a nervous energy rather than a confident, open energy. When you walk from one area to another, do so slowly and while standing tall. Stop to make your point or tell a story, then move slowly to another part of the stage before stopping again to elaborate on a different point. When someone asks a question from the opposite side of the room, walk slowly in their direction, acknowledging their presence while listening and approaching their side of the room. So long as people can still hear you, it is a good idea to walk into the audience from time to time—provided you have a purpose for doing so, such as answering a question during an activity that you assigned to the audience.

When you stand, do so with your feet comfortably but firmly planted about shoulder-width apart. You should not stand like a cowboy about ready to draw his guns, but neither should you stand with your legs together as if standing at attention. Standing at attention or with your legs crossed demonstrates a closed, defensive, or uncertain attitude. These positions, which are unnatural ways to stand when we are relaxed, make you a bit unstable and project weakness to others. About the only thing worse than standing on a stage with your legs crossed is doing so while leaning against the lectern. At best, it looks sloppy. At worst, it projects an image of weakness.

When we get nervous, most of us tend to speed up our movements, including hand gestures. If you want to project a more calm, relaxed, and natural image to the audience, remind yourself to slow everything down.

Face the Audience

Even if you are projecting visuals behind you, there is no need to turn your head to look back. Even if you gesture toward the screen, stand so that your shoulders are facing in the direction of the audience. If you keep your shoulders pointed toward the front, you will naturally turn your head back toward the audience without thinking about it after you glance at the screen. Turning slightly and briefly toward the screen to point out a detail is acceptable. However, continually looking at the screen as a reminder of where you are is very distracting and unnecessary. Except in rare incidents, if you use a computer to project visuals, you can place the computer down low in front of you so there is little reason to turn around.

MIT's Hiroshi Ishii faces the audience at TEDxTokyo. (Photo: TEDxTokyo/Andy McGovern.)

Connect with Eye Contact

Related to the importance of facing the audience is establishing good eye contact. Maintaining natural eye contact with the audience is crucial, which is one of the reasons I advise against reading a script or relying on notes—it's hard to look into people's eyes when your eyes are looking down at notes. Your eye contact should appear natural, and you achieve this by looking at actual people in the room. If you instead gaze out at the back of the room or to a point on either side of the room, your audience will detect this at some level and the connection will be weakened.

If your audience is relatively small, say, under 50 or so, it may be possible to actually look everyone in the eye at some point during your talk as you move deliberately to different parts of the room. For larger audiences in a typical keynote-style presentation, it is still useful to pick out actual people to lock eyes with as you speak—even people who are sitting toward the back. By looking at one person, others near that person will feel as if you are looking at them as well. This is a technique that professional singers use when playing larger halls. It is important not to just glance at or scan general areas of a room but rather to briefly establish actual eye contact with people in different parts of the room.

Put Energy in Your Voice

It's true that the best presentations seem more like good conversations, but there is a difference between speaking with two or three people over coffee and standing to present to an auditorium of 500 people after lunch. Your tone should be conversational, but your energy must be cranked up several notches. If you are enthusiastic, the energy will help project your voice. Mumbling is absolutely not permitted, and neither is shouting. Shouting is usually not sustainable and it's very unpleasant for the audience. When you shout, the volume may go up but the richness of your voice, the peaks and valleys of your unique intonation, are lost. So stand tall, speak up, and articulate clearly, but be careful not to let your speaking evolve into shouting as you speak with energy and project your voice.

Should you use a mic? If your room is a regular-size classroom or conference room with space for only 10 to 30 people, then a mic may not be necessary. But in almost every other case, a microphone is a good idea. Remember, it is not about you, it is about them. Giving the audience even just a slight bump in volume through the use of a microphone will make it easier for them to hear you. Many presenters, especially men, eschew a mic and decide to shout instead. It's as if declining a microphone and choosing to shout is somehow more manly and assertive. But unless you are a head coach delivering an inspiring halftime speech for your football team, shouting is a very bad idea. You are not addressing your troops, remember, you are trying to present in a natural, conversational manner. The microphone, far from being a barrier to connection, can actually be a great enabler of intimacy as it allows you to project in your best and most engaging natural voice.

Only use a handheld mic, however, for very short speeches and announcements. A better option than a handheld mic is a wireless lavalier mic, also called a clip-on or lapel mic. The lavalier is good because it frees up a hand, which is especially important if your other hand is holding a remote control device. The downside of a lavalier is that if you turn your head to the side, some mics will not pick up your voice as well. Whenever possible, the best type of microphone to use is the headband or headset variety used for conferences such as TED. This type of wireless mic places the tiny tip of the mic just to the side of your mouth or your cheek and is virtually invisible to the audience. The advantage of this mic, besides eliminating the possibility of ruffling noises from your shirt, is that no matter how you move your head, the mic stays in the same position and always picks up your voice clearly.

Master game creator Tetsuya Mizuguchi speaking at TEDxTokyo 2011. The wireless headset mic picks up the voice best and allows for freedom of movement.

Don't Read a Speech

Communications guru Bert Decker urges speakers to avoid reading a speech whenever possible. In his book *You've Got to Be Believed to Be Heard,* Decker advises against reading speeches. "Reading is boring," he says. "Worse, reading a speech makes the speaker look inauthentic and unenthusiastic." This goes for reading slides as well. Many years ago the typical use of slideware involved people actually reading lines of text right from the slides behind them—and believe it or not, it still happens today. But don't do it. Putting lots of text on a slide and then reading that text is a great way to alienate your audience and ruin any hope you have of making a connection.

Guy Kawasaki, a venture capitalist and former chief evangelist at Apple, urges people to use large type on slides that people can actually see. "This forces you, he says, "to actually know your presentation and just put the core of the text on your slide." This is what the outspoken Kawasaki had to say about reading text off slides in a speech he gave to a room full of entrepreneurs in Silicon Valley in 2006:

> "If you need to put eight-point or ten-point fonts up there, it's because you do not know your material. If you start reading your material because you do not know your material, the audience is very quickly going to think that you are a bozo. They are going to say to themselves 'This bozo is reading his slides. I can read faster than this bozo can speak. I will just read ahead.'"

Guy's comments got a lot of laughs, but he's right. If you plan on reading slides, you might as well call off the presentation now, because your ability to connect with, persuade, or teach the audience anything will approach zero. Reading slides is no way to show presence, make a connection, or even transfer information in a memorable way. In many cases, reading a deck of slides is indeed a good way to put the room to sleep.

Images in the slides above from iStockphoto.com

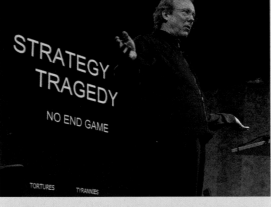

If Your Idea is Worth Spreading...

The annual TED (Technology, Entertainment, Design) conference brings together the world's most fascinating thinkers and doers, who are invited to give insanely great talks on stage in 18 minutes or less. The time limit usually results in very concise, tight, and focused talks. If you have ideas worth talking about, then you've got to be able to stand, deliver, and make your case. As the presenters at TED demonstrate every year, presentation skill is critically important.

What's great about TED is that their amazing presentations are not limited to an elite few. Instead, they "give it away" by uploading tons of their best presentations to the Web and making the videos available in many different formats for online viewing and downloading. Hundreds of quality short-form presentations from the TED archives are available online, and more are added each week. The production quality is excellent and so is the content. TED truly exemplifies the spirit of the conceptual age—share, give it away, make it easy—because the more people who know your idea, the more powerful it becomes. Because of the high-quality free videos, the reach and impact of TED is huge. The TED website is a great resource for content and for those interested in watching good presentations, often with good use of multimedia.

www.ted.com/talks

Al Gore **TOP**
(TED/ leslieimage.com)

William McDonough **CENTER**
(TED/ Asa Mathat)

Sir Ken Robinson **BOTTOM**
(TED/ leslieimage.com)

Stand, Deliver, Connect

Hans Rosling (right), a professor of global health at Sweden's Karolinska Institute, is the Zen master of presenting statistics that have meaning and  tell a story. Rosling co-developed the software behind his visualizations through his nonprofit Gapminder. Using U.N. statistics, Rosling shows that it is indeed a different world. Several presentations on the TED website showcase Rosling's talents. Conventional wisdom says to never stand between the screen and the projector, which is generally good advice. But as you can see from the photo here, Rosling at times defies conventional wisdom and gets involved with the data in an energetic way that engages his audience with the data and the story.

Other TED presenters on this page demonstrate the importance of standing front and center and connecting with the audience.

Hans Rosling (*TED/ leslieimage.com*)

June Cohen
(*TED/ leslieimage.com*)

John Doerr
(*TED/ leslieimage.com*)

Lawrence Lessig
(*TED/ leslieimage.com*)

Carolyn Porco
(*TED/ leslieimage.com*)

Hara Hachi Bu:
Why Length Matters

A consequence of Zen practice is increased attentiveness to the present, a calmness, and an ability to focus on the here and now. However, for your average audience member, it is a safe bet that he or she is not completely "calm" or present in the "here and now." Instead, your audience member is processing many emotional opinions and juggling several issues at the moment—both professional and personal—while doing his or her best to listen to you. We all struggle with this. It is virtually impossible for our audience to concentrate completely on what we are saying, even for shorter presentations. Many studies show that concentration really takes a hit after 15 to 20 minutes. My experience tells me it's less than that. For example, CEOs have notoriously short attention spans while listening to a presentation. So the length of your presentation matters.

Every case is different, but generally, shorter is better. But why then do so many presenters go past their allotted time—or, worse, milk a presentation to stretch it out to the allotted time, even when it seems that the points have pretty much been made? This is probably a result of much of our formal education. I can still hear my college philosophy professor saying before the two-hour in-class written exam: "Remember, more is better." As students, we grow up in an atmosphere that perpetuates the idea that a 20-page paper will likely get a higher grade than a 10-page paper, and a one-hour presentation with 25 presentation slides filled with 12-point lines of text shows more hard work than a 30-minute presentation with 50 highly visual slides. This old-school thinking does not take into account the creativity, intellect, and forethought that it takes to achieve a clarity of ideas. We take this "more is better" thinking with us into our professional lives.

One Secret to a Healthy Life (and a Great Presentation)

The Japanese have a great expression concerning healthy eating habits: *hara hachi bu,* which means "eat until 80 percent full." This is excellent advice, and it's pretty easy to follow this principle in Japan since portions are generally much smaller than in places like the United States. Using chopsticks also makes it easier to avoid shoveling food in and encourages a bit slower pace.

This principle does not encourage wastefulness; it does not mean to leave 20 percent of your meal on the plate. (In fact, it is bad form to leave food on your plate.) In Japan and Asia in general, we usually order as a group and then take only what we need from the shared bounty. I have found—ironically, perhaps—that if I stop eating before getting full, I am more satisfied with the meal. I'm not sleepy after lunch or dinner, and I generally feel much better.

The principle of hara hachi bu also applies to the length of speeches, presentations, and even meetings. My advice is this: No matter how much time you are given, never ever go over your allotted time; in fact, finish a bit before your time is up. How long you talk will depend on your unique situation at the time, but try to shoot for 90 to 95 percent of your allotted time. No one will complain if you finish with a few minutes to spare. The problem with most presentations is that they are too long, not that they are too short.

Leave Them Just a Little Hungry (for More)

Professional entertainers know that you want to end on a high note and leave the audience yearning for just a bit more from you. We want to leave our audiences satisfied—motivated, inspired, more knowledgeable—not feeling that they could have done with just a little less.

We can apply this spirit to the length and amount of material we put into presentations as well. Give them high quality—the highest you can—but do not give them so much quantity that you leave them with their heads spinning and guts aching.

This is a typical ekiben (a special boxed meal sold at train stations) from one of my trips to Tokyo. Simple. Appealing. Economic in scale. Nothing superfluous. Made with the "honorable passenger" in mind. After spending 20 or 30 minutes savoring the contents of the ekiben, complemented by Japanese beer, I'm left happy, nourished, and satisfied, but not full. I could eat more—another perhaps—but I do not need to. Indeed, I do not want to. I am satisfied with the experience. Eating to the point of becoming full would only destroy the quality of the experience I'm having.

Every word that is unnecessary only pours over the side of a brimming mind.

— Cicero

In Sum

- You need solid content and logical structure, but you also have to make a connection with the audience. You must appeal to both the logical and the emotional sides of your audience members.

- If your content is worth talking about, then bring energy and passion to your delivery. Every situation is different, but there is never an excuse to be dull.

- Don't hold back. If you have a passion for your topic, then let people know it.

- Make a strong start with PUNCH. Include content that is personal, unexpected, novel, challenging, or humorous to make a connection from the beginning.

- Project yourself well by dressing the part, moving with confidence and purpose, maintaining good eye contact, and speaking in a conversational style but with elevated energy.

- Try not to read a presentation or rely on notes.

- Remember the concept of *hara hachi bu.* It is better to leave your audience satisfied yet yearning for a bit more, than to leave them stuffed and feeling that they have had more than enough.

10

The Need for Engagement

We say that the best presenters and public speakers are the ones who engage their audiences the most. We praise the best teachers for being able to engage their students. With or without multimedia, engagement is key. Yet if you ask a hundred people for a definition of engagement, you'll get a hundred different answers. So what is engagement? For me, regardless of the topic, engagement is, at its core, about emotion. The need to appeal to people's emotions is fundamental, yet often neglected. It's about the emotions of the speaker and his or her ability to express those emotions in a sincere manner. But mostly, engagement is about tapping the emotions of the audience to get them involved on a personal level with the material, whatever it may be.

Like it or not, we are emotional beings. Logic is necessary, but rarely sufficient. We must appeal to people's right brains, or creative sides, as well. Here's what the authors of *Why Business People Speak Like Idiots* (Free Press) say:

> *"In business, our natural instincts are always left-brained. We create tight arguments and knock the audience into submission with facts, figures, historical graphs, and logic…. The bad news is that the barrage of facts often works against you. My facts against your experiences, emotions, and perceptual filters. Not a fair fight—facts will lose every time."*

We really have our work cut out for us. Our audiences bring their own emotions, experiences, biases, and perceptual filters that are no match for data and facts alone. We must be careful not to make the mistake of thinking that our data can speak for itself, no matter how convincing, obvious, or strong it may seem to us. We may indeed have the best product or solid research, but if we plan a dull, dispassionate, "death by slideument" snooze-fest, we will lose. The best presenters engage by tapping people's emotions.

Emotions and Memory

Reaching people at an emotional level can get attention, but it can also help your material be remembered. If you can arouse the emotions of your audience with a relevant story, an interesting (and relevant) activity, or a remarkable image or piece of data—for example, that is unexpected, surprising, sad, disturbing, and so on—your material will be better remembered. When a member of your audience experiences an emotionally charged event in your presentation, the amygdala in the limbic system of the brain releases dopamine into that person's system. And dopamine, says *Brain Rules* author Dr. John Medina, "greatly helps with memory and information processing."

In a sales situation, for example, ask yourself what it is that you're really selling. It's not the features or the thing itself but the experience of the thing and all the emotions related to it that you are really selling. For example, if you were selling mountain bikes, would you focus on the features of mountain bikes or would you focus on the experience of using the bikes? Stories of experiences are vivid and visual and bring people's emotions into your narrative.

Mirror Neurons

A mirror neuron in the brain fires both when you do something and when you see someone else doing the same thing, even though you have not moved. It's almost as if you, the observer, are actually engaging in the same behavior as the person who is engaged in the action. Watching something and doing something are not the same, of course, but as far as our brains are concerned, they're pretty darn close.

Mirror neurons may be involved in empathy as well. This is a crucial survival skill. Research has shown that the same area of the brain that lights up when a person experiences an emotion also activates when that person merely sees someone else experiencing that emotion. When we see someone express passion, joy, concern, and the like, experts believe the mirror neurons send messages to the limbic region of the brain, the area associated with emotion. In a sense, then, there is a place in the brain that seems to be responsible for living in other people's brains—that is, to feel what they are feeling.

I use the two slides above in a marketing presentation to remind people to think again about what it is they are really selling. Is it the thing or the experience of the thing? (Images in slides from iStockphoto.com.)

If we are wired to feel what others feel, is it any wonder that people get bored and disinterested when listening to someone who seems bored and disinterested, even though the content may be useful? Is it any wonder we feel stiff and uncomfortable while watching someone on stage barely move a muscle except for the muscles that make the mouth open and close? Too many presentations today are still given in an overly formal, static, and didactic style that removes the visual component, including the visual messages expressed through movement and displays of emotion. An animated, natural display of emotions enriches our narrative as it stimulates others to unconsciously feel what we feel. When you are passionate, for example, so long as it is perceived as genuine, most people will mirror that emotion back. Our data and our evidence matter, but the genuine emotions we project have a direct and strong influence—for good and for bad—on the message our audience ultimately receives and remembers.

Power of the Smile

Smiles are contagious, yet they must be real. You can try to fake a smile, but people can tell when you don't mean it. In fact, some studies show that if you give an insincere smile, audiences may perceive you as projecting an untrustworthy or hypocritical image. Martin Seligman, author of *Authentic Happiness,* says there are essentially two types of smiles, the "Duchenne smile" and the "Pan American smile." The Duchenne smile is the genuine smile, characterized by movement of the muscles around the mouth and also the eyes. You can tell a real smile by how the skin around the eyes wrinkles up a bit. The Pan American smile is the fake smile that involves voluntary movement around the mouth only. This is the polite smile you see from people in the service industry who are doing their best but not having a great day.

We can all recognize an insincere smile. But a presenter or entertainer who actually looks happy to be there (because he or she really is) is well on the way to engaging the audience naturally. Genuine smiles show that we are happy to be there. And since people in our audience can feel what we feel, why wouldn't we want them to feel at ease? While you may think it's only your words that people should remember, your audience will actually recall much of what they saw, including your facial expressions, and what they felt.

純粋な笑顔の力

Photo in slide: Jiji

The slide above (16:9 aspect ratio) features a full-screen image of Miwa Yoshida and Masa Nakamura from the legendary Japanese pop group Dreams Come True. I mention them often in Japanese seminars because I have never seen a duo display more energy and infectious, genuine smiles on stage than these two. Performing music for three hours in front of 60,000 people is different than making a presentation, of course, but these activities share the same essence. We must engage by being completely in the moment, connected, and engaged with this particular audience. The interest and passion we show though our genuine smiles and laughter will go a long way toward that meaningful engagement. (The text on the slide translates to the "Power of a genuine smile.")

Stimulate Their Curiosity

Famed physicist Michio Kaku says "We are born scientists." What he means is we are all born insanely curious creatures—that's how we learn. Showing your curiosity and stimulating it in others is a powerful emotion for engagement. Curiosity can be ignited and stimulated by a good presentation or it can be all but extinguished by a poor presentation. Most business presentations today fail to stimulate the curiosity of the audience members because they are dull, one-way information dumps.

Maybe this is something we learned in school, at least starting from our secondary-school days. From my experience, and based on the countless e-mails I get from teachers around the world, the problem today in many schools is that the methods of instruction do a poor job of nurturing students' natural curiosity. This is nothing new. Einstein said many years ago that "it is in fact nothing short of a miracle that the modern methods of instruction have not yet entirely strangled the holy curiosity of inquiry." Children go through much of their childhood driven by a natural and insatiable curiosity, but as Dr. Kaku says, in too many cases the methods of instruction in schools result in "crushing curiosity right out of the next generation."

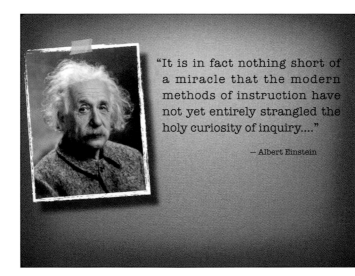

"It is in fact nothing short of a miracle that the modern methods of instruction have not yet entirely strangled the holy curiosity of inquiry...."

— Albert Einstein

Kenichiro Mogi, a famous brain scientist in Japan, says the curiosity of a child is something we must keep with us always. We must keep our sense of wonder he insists. "By forgetting how to be curious we are losing something really valuable. Because curiosity is the single most important trait that brought us here today." The best presenters and the best teachers are the ones who demonstrate their curiosity and passionate interest in their subjects. A presenter who demonstrates his own passionate curiosity inspires and cultivates the natural curiosity in others. You can't fake curiosity and wonder. The best teachers guide, coach, inspire, and feed that natural flame of curiosity that lives within every child. The best presenters are the ones who are not afraid to show their unbridled curiosity and passionate sense of wonder about their work.

Curiosity is Infectious

A good example of a person who presents important information with an infectious sense of curiosity and wonder is Swedish medical doctor Hans Rosling. Yes, Hans's Gapminder-powered data visualizations are very compelling on stage. However, he shows his passionate curiosity and engages his audiences by the way he speaks, with exclamations such as:

Do you see that?
Look here!
This is amazing!
What do you think happens next?
Wasn't that surprising?

This is the kind of language that engages the listener. Hans Rosling brings the data alive through visualizations, and taps people's emotions by putting the information in the context of a story, making it accessible to all who will listen. He also brings his own brand of dry humor, and humor is one of the most powerful forms of emotional engagement of all.

Engagement is Not About Tools

Many people talk about technology as if it is a panacea for boring and ineffective presentations. Digital tools have, in many ways, increased the quality of communication and engagement for live presentations. This is especially true when engaging with people live on the other side of the planet via tools such as video conferencing, webinars, Skype, and so on. Yet, while our technology has evolved in dramatic ways over the last generation, our fundamental human need for connection, engagement, and relationships has not changed. Companies today promote their bells and whistles and whizzing animations as elements that are guaranteed to engage. However, we should be very skeptical about such claims. The use of more and more tools and effects often leads to distraction.

Eiji Han Shimizu is a Japanese filmmaker and creator of the award-winning film *Happy*. In his 2011 TEDxTokyo presentation, Shimizu underscored the idea that it is not always more that makes us happy, but rather it is the intentional selection of less, an aesthetic at the heart of traditional Japanese culture. "A blind march toward progress that's based on distraction, temptation, and consumption may not bring happiness," Shimizu says. Applying this sentiment to the modern age of presentation technology and digital tools, we could say that too many of us are marching to accept loads of software effects, tricks, and techniques in the name of "progress" and "engagement." As more digital tools become available at a faster pace, it may be the intentional selection of less that actually leads to the most engagement and the best presentations.

No matter what the digital toolmakers say, engagement is much more about you and your ideas, not about software features and presentation techniques. (Image in slide above from IStockphoto.com.)

Gihan Perera

Author of the best-selling book *Webinar Smarts: The Smart Way for Professional Speakers, Trainers, Thought Leaders and Business Professionals to Deliver Engaging and Profitable Webinars.*
www.webinarsmarts.com

Webinar expert Gihan Perera offers advice on how to run an effective webinar that engages people.

Webinars (seminars delivered over the Internet) are very popular today, both for promotional and educational purposes. They cost very little to prepare and present, and save travel time and costs for both you and your participants.

They do have some traps for the unwary, though—even if you are an experienced presenter. You have to put more work into your presentation slides, manage the energy of the audience differently, and operate the technology competently.

Here are seven techniques for being more effective and engaging in a webinar.

1. Be relevant.

If I conducted a webinar that guaranteed to tell you the winning numbers for next weekend's lottery, I would have your attention even with scratchy audio, a slow Internet connection, busy slides, bullet points, clip art, and ugly fonts! So understand your audience, and solve their problems, answer their questions, and add value. Substance trumps style every time. But don't settle for one or the other—excel at both.

This is especially important for webinars, because webinar audiences want information and education. They don't come to be motivated, inspired, or entertained (it's a bonus if they get that as well). Rather, they come for rock-solid takeaway value they can use to tackle their questions, challenges, problems, and aspirations.

2. Use more slides.

In a face-to-face presentation, your slides are a visual aid; in a webinar, they are the visuals. So use more slides than you normally would. This keeps your audience's interest and provides visual reinforcement to your words.

Broadly, each slide should match what you're talking about at the time (much more so than in a face-to-face presentation, where some slides can be just a backdrop). If you really want a number, then aim for roughly one slide per minute.

3. Be elegant with your design.

Diamonds are beautiful, pearls are elegant. In your webinar slides, aim for simple elegance rather than striking beauty. Use diagrams and models rather than bulleted lists; smaller photographs rather than full-screen pictures; plain backgrounds rather than corporate templates; and icons rather than words.

4. "Build" your slides.

Build up your complex slides as you're talking about them. If you're showing a graph, start with the axes, then the labels, then the bars or lines, then the highlighted points. If you're showing a model, build it up step by step.

It's easy to do this in PowerPoint using the Custom Animation feature (but don't use fancy animation—just let each part "appear"). Or, simply use a series of slides that build up to the final picture.

5. Get them active.

Make your webinars active and interactive. Your audience is attending a live event, so involve them in it.

Ask them to do something simple early in your presentation. This forces them to take notice, involves them right from the start, and demonstrates that this isn't just another boring presentation. For example, you could conduct a poll, pose a puzzle, ask them to write something, or ask some people to speak out loud (but only if you've asked for permission beforehand).

6. Shift energy.

As with any other presentation, design segments that shift the energy during the webinar. For example:

- Conduct online polls.
- Ask them to write or draw things.
- Stop talking for 30 seconds of reflection time.
- Show a list and ask them to mentally pick their top three priorities.
- Ask for questions.
- Hand the presentation over to a guest presenter.
- Switch from a slide show to a Web page or some other software.

Hint: Don't do all these things in your first webinar. Build up to them over time, as you become more familiar with the technology.

7. Start before you're ready.

Webinars can be unsettling and nerve-wracking, even for experienced presenters. The only solution to this is practice. Take the pressure off yourself by starting small. Start with small groups, not large audiences. Offer free webinars before you start charging money. Get somebody else to manage the technology for you. Write a script for what you're going to say.

But whatever you do: Start!

Avoid bulleted slides like the first slide above—they are just not engaging. The third example is great for a live keynote-style talk, but the images will not load well in a webinar. The center example is much more visual than a bulleted list, yet it will also load quickly in a webinar. If you do use a beautiful, large photo, just be aware that it will take a few moments to appear.

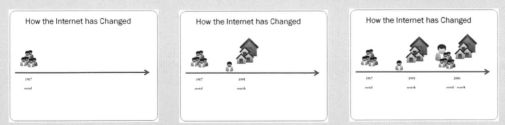

You can keep people engaged with your screen and your narrative if you build your visuals. You can do this using animation features in your software or just use separate slides as illustrated above.

Remove Barriers to Communication

I'm not a fan of the lectern (also referred to as the podium). Yes, it has its place, and sometimes its use is unavoidable. But in almost every speaking situation, standing behind a lectern is like standing behind a wall.

Lecterns can make a speaker look authoritative and in command. This is why politicians love speaking from behind them. If you aim to look "large and in charge," then perhaps a lectern is appropriate for you. But for most of us—conference presenters, teachers, sales reps, etc.—the last place we want to be is behind a wall. Also, lecterns are often placed to the side and back from the edge of the stage. In this case, you are not only behind a barrier, any visuals you use are the main focus and your physical presence is very much diminished. It's possible for both you and the screen to be front and center, which is where people are naturally going to focus their attention.

If you present from behind a lectern, you may, more or less, sound the same and the media may look the same, but it's not ideal. In fact, it's far from ideal. The connection is lost. Imagine if your favorite singer performed from behind a lectern. Ridiculous, of course. Imagine, too, if Steve Jobs had given his famous keynotes with the same slides and same video clips, same jeans and black turtleneck, but did all the talking from behind a lectern. He might have sounded the same. The visuals might have looked the same. But the connection and engagement would not be there.

Generally, the lectern is "so last millennium," but there are times when its use is perfectly acceptable, such as when multiple speakers take turns at center stage during a formal ceremony. Graduation ceremonies are a good example. But when people have walked in that room specifically to hear you, learn from you, and be convinced or inspired by you, then you've got to do whatever you can to remove all walls—literally and figuratively—between you and the audience. It's scary, and takes practice, but it will make all the difference.

A very common scene is shown above. Note the three levels of barriers: First, there is the lectern. Then, there is the computer screen. Finally, there is the ream of notes the presenter is holding. These three items act as walls between the presenter and the audience. The fact that she will be looking down to read and speaking in a more formal, less conversational language, will not help her engagement either. Remove the walls—all of them—as much as possible.

Redux: Presentation Lessons from Steve Jobs

On the morning of October 6, 2011, I sat down at the kitchen counter at our home in Nara, Japan, with a cup of coffee and turned on the news to check the day's weather forecast. Instead the network issued a special report from the U.S.: "Steve Jobs has died." My heart sank.

Except for a couple of e-mails and occasionally saying hello to Steve at the Cafe Macs's salad bar on the Apple campus in Cupertino, I never had much direct contact with him while I worked at Apple. Still, I was deeply, deeply saddened by the news of his passing. If truth be told, it was Steve's special ability to connect and engage a large audience in such a natural and simple way that first attracted me to Apple a generation ago. I had read all the public speaking and presentation books over the years, of course, but it was Steve Jobs's presentation skills from which I learned the most by far.

I saw virtually every keynote presentation Steve Jobs ever made since 1997 (and all the archived videos before then), and while I was with Apple I never missed a special employee event or town hall meeting on campus. Although I touched on lessons from Steve Jobs a few times earlier in this book, what follows is a summary of some of the most salient lessons from the master of the keynote presentation.

Know when *not* to use slides.

Multimedia is great for presentations before large groups such as keynote addresses or conference presentations, but in meetings where you want to discuss issues or go over details in depth, slides—especially the bulleted list variety, which are never a good idea—are usually counter productive. Jobs was well known inside Apple for hating slide presentations in meetings. "I hate the way people use slide presentations instead of thinking," Jobs told biographer Walter Isaacson when describing meetings upon his return to Apple in 1997. "People would confront a problem by creating a presentation. I wanted them to engage, to hash things out at the table, rather than show a bunch of slides. People who know what they're talking about don't need PowerPoint."

Jobs preferred to use the whiteboard to explain his ideas and hash out things with people. There is a difference between a keynote and ballroom style presentations (and TED talks and similar events) and a meeting around a conference table. Most productive meetings are a time for discussion and working things out, not simply going through a bunch of slides. Save the multimedia for the larger presentations. The tips below mainly concern presentations for larger audiences.

Remember that even on stage, multimedia is not always needed.

In cases where you want to create more of a town hall feel and generate discussion with the audience, consider pulling up a stool at the front of the stage to tell your story. The few times that I saw Steve Jobs address employees in the Town Hall Auditorium at 4 Infinite Loop in Cupertino, he did not use multimedia, and instead sat on a stool at the center of the stage to give his report and field questions. This instantly felt more like a conversation. As much as I love multimedia, sometimes it just does not fit the occasion.

Be very clear and very focused.
In the preparation stage you must be ruthless in cutting the superfluous from the talk, both in terms of content and in terms of what visuals you use. Poor presentations, no matter how good the visuals or even delivery may be, result from poor planning and a lack of focus on what your core points are and the key messages that you want people to take a way. Steve Jobs was laser sharp in his focus in almost all business matters, including the planning of his presentations. Focus, as Jobs said when talking about products, means that you often need to say no to things. You can't cover everything in a presentation; have the courage to cut the non-essential. Most presentations that fail do so because they include too much information and display it in a cluttered way that does not engage the brain.

Develop rapport with the audience.
Jobs usually walked out on stage, all smiles, without any formal introduction over the PA. Jobs showed his personality, which was confident but humble and friendly, on stage (an image he did not always project during meetings with his employees). People are attracted to confidence—but it must be confidence, combined with humility. Jobs used natural movement on stage, eye contact, and a subtle friendliness to establish a connection with the audience.

Give them an idea of where you're going.
You do not need an agenda slide, but give people an idea where you're going, a bit of a road map of the journey you're taking them on. In Jobs's case, after a simple, friendly greeting he often began with something like: "I've got four things I'd like to talk about with you today. So let's get started. First..." Jobs often structured his talks around three or four parts with one theme.

Show your enthusiasm.
You may want to tone down your enthusiasm at times, but most presenters show too little passion or enthusiasm, not too much. Each case is unique, but enthusiasm can make all the difference. Jobs's enthusiasm was subtle, but you could detect it in his tone and the words that he chose. In just the first few minutes on stage Jobs often used superlatives such as incredible, extraordinary, awesome, amazing, revolutionary. You can say his language was over the top, but Steve Jobs believed what he said. He was sincere. Yet the point is not to speak like Steve Jobs—or move around like Steve Ballmer—but to find your own level of passion and bring that honest enthusiasm out in your work for the world to see in your own style.

Be positive, upbeat, humorous.
Jobs was a very serious person, but he came across in presentations as an extremely positive person because he deeply believed in his content. He was upbeat and positive about the future, even in hard times. Reality distortion field or not, this positive energy is the image he projected on stage. You cannot fake this—you must believe in your content or you cannot sell it. Jobs also brought a little humor to his talks. This did not mean telling jokes. His humor was more subtle. Making people laugh occasionally through subtle uses of irony is engaging.

Focus not on the numbers, but on what the numbers mean.
A business keynote by a technology company is different from a scientific presentation at a conference. But isn't it always about what the numbers mean rather than just the numbers themselves? So your cholesterol is 199, the national average. Is that good or bad? Up or down? Is "average" healthy or unhealthy? And compared

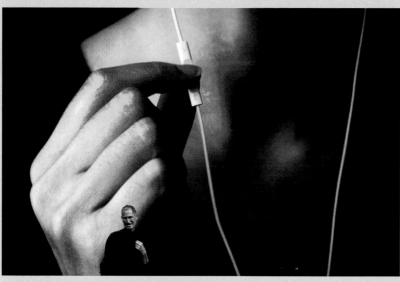

Steve Jobs's keynotes always featured high-impact visuals.

Jobs balanced his high-impact visuals by occasionally having the screen behind him contain no information at all, the equivalent of placing blank slides or spaces in your visual narrative. This places all eyes on you. (Photos on this page by Justin Sullivan/ iStockphoto.com.)

to what? When Steve Jobs talked about numbers in his keynotes, he often broke them down. For example, he may have said something like four million iPhones sold is the equivalent of 20,000 per day since the units went on sale. 20 percent market share? In and of itself that does not mean much, but the meaning becomes clear when he compared it to others in the field. When presenting data, always ask yourself "compared to what?"

Make it visual.

Jobs used huge screens and large, high-quality graphics for his keynotes and special events. The images were clear, professional, and unique, and never from a template. Charts and graphs were simple and beautifully clear. There was never "death by bullet point." Jobs used the screen to show visual material and only occasionally for displaying short lists. He displayed data in a way that the meaning was instantly clear. Not every presentation requires photos or movie clips, but if you do use multimedia, make it simple, yet of high quality.

Introduce something unexpected.

Jobs's presentations always had something new. But he also surprised audiences just a bit each time. Humans love the unexpected. We love some element that makes us go "aah!" The brain loves novelty.

Vary the pace and change techniques.

Jobs was good at varying the pace from fast to slow and changing the flow by using different techniques. He did not stand in one place and lecture, a very bad way to present. Instead, he mixed in video clips, images, stories, data, different speakers, and live hardware and software demos. Just talking about information for one or two hours is much too boring for the audience (and for the presenter). If the talk were only about information and new features, it would be more efficient to give that information out in a handout for people to read when they have the time.

Go the appropriate length.

Jobs never included unnecessary details and finished on time. He was aware that presentations cannot go on too long and got to his points smoothly and quickly. If you cannot explain why your topic is important, interesting, and meaningful in 20 minutes or less, then you do not know your topic well enough. Try to make talks as short as possible while still making the content meaningful, keeping in mind that every case is different. The key is not to fill your audience up; you want them to leave wanting just a little more.

Save the best for last.

People will make an assessment about your performance in the first two minutes, so you have to start strong. But you have to finish even stronger. People best remember the first part and the last part of your presentation. The middle stuff is important, of course, but if you blow it at the beginning or at the end, all may be lost. This is why you have to rehearse your opening and your closing so much. Jobs was famous for his "one more thing" slide where he saved the best for last—after it appeared he was finishing.

Steve Jobs often talked about changing the world, and he *did* change the world in his short 56 years on this planet. His incredible dedication to detail, simplicity, and aesthetics raised the bar for technology, business, design, and beyond. He even raised the bar for presentations. In spite of his mercurial nature, he was a true master. He was a true sensei.

When Jobs showed numbers, they were big and impossible to miss. In this photo taken at Macworld 2008 in San Francisco, he is announcing that over five million copies of Mac OS 10.5 were purchased since its release. (Photo by David Paul Morris/ iStockphoto.com.)

Jobs always made good use of images to compare and contrast features. In this photo he is introducing a new iPod Nano during an Apple special event in 2007 in San Francisco. (Photo by Justin Sullivan/ iStockphoto.com.)

Get Close to the Audience

My experience teaching and presenting in different parts of the world over the past 20 years has taught me that the physical distance between a speaker and the audience—and the distance between the audience members—has a great influence on the ability to engage and be effective. The spatial context has a great impact on nonverbal communication and the quality of engagement. Ideas concerning personal space vary among cultures, but as much as possible, engaging an audience means being close to the audience. In addition, it helps if your audience members are close to each other. Within physical limitations, as a general principle we must (1) shorten the distance between ourselves and the audience, (2) bring individual audience members closer to each other while remaining sensitive to local perceptions of personal space, and (3) remove any barriers between us and the audience that create distance, whether it's actual distance or merely a perception. Perceived distance, for example, is created by using language that is too formal, inappropriate, or industry specific for a particular audience. Technology, too, if not used well can create a feeling of distance that diminishes engagement regardless of how close you may physically be to the audience.

The typical lecture hall like this—with chairs and tables that cannot be moved—does not lend itself to engagement. I took this picture, then worked to modify the room. I set up my computer away from the lectern on the elevated podium, and instead came down closer to the students. While not ideal, it at least removed some of the barriers. We were even able to do some group work in spite of the rigid setup. I further attempted to remove barriers by often walking into the audience, especially during the short activities.

Even modern, beautiful halls like the one at Akita University shown above typically place a large lectern at the front. You can see that we cleared the lectern to the side, making room on stage for me to walk. At right, I placed the computer down low and completely out of sight of the audience.

In the large auditorium shown at left, I moved the lectern off the stage and moved down to the front row. In this position I can see the computer without the audience being aware that I am glancing at a monitor from time to time. Note in this photo that the audience members are speaking to each other. As much as possible, I try to get the audience to connect with each other, not just with me.

Use a Small Remote to Advance Visuals

I see a lot of presentations given by very smart people. Despite their intelligence, all too often presenters use a remote poorly (as if it's the first time they've seen such a device) or not at all. Even today, too many presenters stay next to the computer on a table or lectern or walk back to the computer to change slides every few minutes.

Remote control devices for computers are relatively cheap and an absolute must. No excuses, you've got to have one. If you are not currently using a remote to advance slides, adding one to your delivery style will make a huge difference. The remote allows you to get out front closer to the people, move to different parts of the stage or room, and make those connections.

When we stay glued to the laptop and look down to advance every slide, our presentations become more like slide shows with narration—the kind your uncle used to bore you with when he whipped out his 35mm slide projector with highlights of his latest fishing trip. Yawn.

Remember, you want the technology behind your presentation to be as invisible as possible to the audience. If you use technology well, your audience will not even know (or care) what actual digital tools you are using. But when you have your hand on the computer and your eyes are moving back and forth from the computer screen to the keyboard to the audience or projection screen, it becomes more like the typical slide presentations that people complain about.

If you are giving the kind of presentation that requires a computer for more than simply advancing slides, then it's fine to occasionally go to the computer to start a program, demonstrate a website, and so on. However, you should also move away from the computer when you do not have to be there.

A small and basic remote is all you need. I prefer small remotes with only the most basic features. You can buy remotes that you can mouse around with on screen and are equipped with myriad other features, but they are large and call attention to themselves. All you really need is the ability to advance, go back, and turn the screen black. Very simple.

Use the B Key

If you use slideware in presentations, one of the most useful keys to remember is the B key. If you hit the B key in PowerPoint or Keynote, your screen becomes black. (Pressing the W key creates a white screen.) You can even build black screens into your presentation by inserting black slides at various points in your talk when you want to shift all attention away from the screen. Hitting the B key is very useful, for example, if a spontaneous but relevant discussion diverges a bit from the visual information on the screen. Changing the screen to black removes information that may have become a distraction and puts all eyes on you and the people engaged in the discussion. When you are ready to proceed further with your prepared points, just hit the B key again (this feature is on most remote controls as well) and the slides display again.

Filmmaker Kaori Brand keeps her eyes on the TEDxTokyo audience and advances her visuals smoothly with the remote (in her right hand) as if there were nothing in her hand at all. The best presenters get comfortable with the remote and use their hands naturally, never calling attention to the piece of plastic in their hand. (Photo: TEDxTokyo/Andy McGovern.)

Leave the Lights On

If you are going to engage an audience, they have to be able to see you. When the audience can actually see your eye movements and read your facial expressions, they will better understand your message. The audience members are interpreting meaning based on verbal (your actual words), vocal (your voice), and visual (your nonverbal language) cues. Your nonverbal signals are a very important part of your message, but if people cannot see you—even if they can see the screen fine—much of the richness of your message will be lost. So while it is tempting to turn the lights off to make the visuals look better, the most important thing is to keep the light on the presenter. Often, a compromise can be worked out by dimming only some of the lights.

Given the advances in projection technology, it is often possible to keep all or most of the lights on in conference rooms and lecture halls today. Auditoriums usually have better lighting setups that can keep lights on the presenter but off the screen. No matter what kind of presentation situation you are in, make sure there is plenty of light on you. You cannot engage the audience members if they cannot see you.

In corporate meeting rooms across Japan, common practice is to turn off all or most of the lights for presentations. It is also very common for the presenter to sit next to or behind a table and operate a computer while the audience stares at the screen and the "presenter" narrates the slides. This practice is so common that it is considered normal. It may be normal, but it is not effective. Audiences better understand the presenter's message when they can both hear *and see* the presenter.

If you turn off the lights and present from the back of the room like this...

...your room will quickly begin to look like this.

How Do You Know When You Are Engaging?

When you truly engage someone in a presentation, you can awaken something inside them. Benjamin Zander, introduced in Chapter 8, is the master of awakening the possibilities in others. And awakening the possibilities in others—our students, colleagues, audiences, etc.—is exactly what he urges us to do as well. After all, what is the role of a good leader if not to awaken the possibility of a group, organization, or even nation? What is the role of a good teacher if not to inspire and awaken the potential of each student? Is not the role of a good parent—among a million other things—to awaken the possibilities within each of their children? Obviously not every presentation is an opportunity to inspire in a big way, but we need to affect a change in people, and that involves engaging them and awakening them to new possibilities.

How do you know if you are awaking the possibility in each student or audience member, Ben asks. The answer? "Look at their eyes. If their eyes are shining, you know you're doing it." He goes on to say, "If the eyes are not shining you have to ask yourself a question: Who am I being that my players' eyes are not shining?" This goes for our children, students, audience members, and so on. For me, that's the greatest takeaway question: Who am I being when I am not seeing a connection in the eyes of others?

In Sum

- Engagement invloves tapping the audience members' emotions.

- Keep the lights on; the audience must always be able to see you.

- Remove any barriers between you and the audience. Avoid podiums and lecterns, if possible.

- Use a wireless mic and remote control for advancing slides so you can move around freely and naturally.

- Be positive, upbeat, humorous, and develop rapport with the audience. You must believe in your content or you cannot sell it.

next step

What we think, we become.

—Buddha

11

The Journey Begins

Many people look for the short road and the quick fix to achieve presentation excellence. But it doesn't exist—there are no panaceas or off-the-shelf fixes. Learning to become an exceptional presenter in today's world is a journey. This journey offers many paths to presenting in a more enlightened way, a way that is appropriate for the world in which we live. The first step down the road to becoming a great presenter is simply seeing—really seeing—that what passes for normal, ordinary, and good enough is off-kilter with how we learn, understand, remember, and engage.

No matter what your starting point is today, you can become much better. In fact, you can become extraordinary. I know this is true because I have seen it many times before. I have worked with professionals—young and old— who believed they were not particularly creative, charismatic, or dynamic. And yet, with a little help, they were able to transform themselves into extremely creative, highly articulate, engaging presenters once they realized that a remarkable presenter was inside them already. Once they opened their eyes and made the commitment to learn and leave the past behind, it was just a matter of time before great progress was visible. Interestingly, as their confidence grew and they became more effective presenters, their newly found confidence and perspective had a remarkable impact on other aspects of their personal and professional lives.

How to Improve

There are many things you can do to become a better presenter—with or without the use of multimedia—and a better, more effective communicator in general. The following are just a few things to keep in mind.

Read and Study

Through books, DVDs, and myriad online resources, you can teach yourself much of what you need to be an exceptional presenter. On my website, www.presentationzen.com, I recommend many books, DVDs, and websites related to presentation design and delivery. Most of the items I recommend are not necessarily about presentation skills or slideware. However, these are the resources that are often the most helpful. For example, you can learn a lot about storytelling and the use of imagery by studying the masters of documentary film and cinema. Even books on writing screenplays offer lessons you can apply to the world of presentations. You just never know what you'll learn through self-study, especially when you look in unusual places.

Do or Do Not

Reading and studying are important and necessary, but to really get better at presenting—including designing the visuals—you have to actually *do it*, and do it often. So look for opportunities to present. If there is a local Toastmasters (www.toastmasters.org) chapter in your area, consider getting involved. Better yet, look for a local TEDx event (www.ted.com/tedx), PechaKucha Night (www.pecha-kucha.org), or Ignite event (ignite.oreilly.com). If you don't find one of these events in your area, then why not start one? Volunteer to present for your school, business, or user group, and look for other opportunities to "give it away" and make a contribution by sharing your information, skill, or story through a presentation in your community.

Finding inspiration in jazz...

Exercise Your Creativity

It's important for working professionals—no matter their field—to stay in touch with and nurture their creative soul. What a waste it would be to ignore one of your passions or talents. Frankly, you just never know where inspiration will come from. Inspiration, clarity, or a new perspective may materialize unforced as you climb a mountain, paint a portrait, photograph a sunset, write a novel...or find your groove while playing with fellow musicians in a downtown nightclub (or garage).

...and the blues...

I no longer play music full time, but I still perform occasionally with local jazz and blues musicians in nightclubs around Osaka. It's so good for the creative spirit to play live and connect with other musicians and with appreciative audiences. Jazz and the blues especially are about connecting and telling a story through the lyrics and music. It's about feelings. Playing the blues or jazz well is similar to making great presentations—it's not about technique. Once you begin to focus on technique, tricks, flash, and making an impression, all is lost. If I never played music, I would miss all those lessons.

Get Out

Nothing great will ever happen to you if you stay in your comfort zone. So as much as you can, get out of your office or school or house and make connections. Look to exercise the right (creative, emotional) side of your brain. "Out there" is where the learning occurs. Challenge yourself and develop your creativity; exercise your creative brain. Take a drama class. Take an art class. Enroll in a seminar. Go to a movie. Go to a concert. Go to a play or a musical. Or just go for an inspirational walk alone.

...and visiting a temple in Kyoto.

Lessons Are All Around You

We can find inspiration and lessons in unexpected places. For example, over the years I've learned a lot about graphic design—what's effective and what's not—during the morning commute on the trains. Trains in Japan are clean, comfortable, and on time. The trains are also full of print advertising hanging from and affixed to every conceivable space. I enjoy scanning the print ads while I commute as it gives me a chance to keep abreast of new products and events while also studying graphic design trends and observing the way graphics are used in print media.

You can learn a lot about fundamental design principles and develop a critical eye through careful examination of the graphic design found in posters, banners, street signs, storefronts, and so on. We usually ignore or take for granted so much of the design in urban settings, but just walking down the street you'll find that the examples from which to learn are all around you. The lessons are everywhere. It's just a matter of seeing.

It's Within You Already

The key is in knowing that it is within you already. Do not rely on technology or other people to make your choices. Most of all, do not let mere habit—and the habits of others—dictate your decisions on how to prepare, design, and ultimately deliver your presentations. The secret is to increase your awareness so you are able to see the world and all the lessons around you. We cannot truly move forward and learn the new if we cling to the old. The essential keys to improvement are simply having an open mind, an open heart, and a willingness to learn, even if we make mistakes in the process. There are many ways to improve and transform yourself. In this chapter, I have mentioned just a few that I hope will be of help to you.

Conclusion

So, what's the conclusion? The conclusion is there is no conclusion—there is only the next step. And that next step is completely up to you. In fact, far from being the conclusion, for many this is still just the beginning. In this book, I have tried to give you a few simple things to think about as you work toward improving your presentation preparation, design, and delivery skills. This book focused on presenting while using multimedia yet the use of multimedia technology is not appropriate for every case. You decide. However, if you *do* use digital tools to produce visuals for your next talk, aim to design and deliver your presentation while allowing the principles of restraint, simplicity, and naturalness to always be your gentle guide. Enjoy the journey.

A journey of a thousand miles
begins with a single step.

—Lao-tzu

Photo Credits

Markuz Wernli Saito

Garden photographs reprinted with permission from the book *Mirei Shigemori, Modernizing The Japanese Garden* (Stone Bridge Press) by Christian Tschumi and Markuz Wernli Saito. See Markuz's portfolio at www.markuz.com.

Introduction   **Chapter 1**

| istockphoto.com | istockphoto.com | istockphoto.com | istockphoto.com | istockphoto.com | istockphoto.com | istockphoto.com | istockphoto.com |
| 2913656 | 000011911622 | 000003223474 | 000016427589 | 000007863302 | 000011421652 | 000001271432 | 000003502193 |

Chapter 2   **Chapter 3**

| istockphoto.com | istockphoto.com | istockphoto.com | istockphoto.com | istockphoto.com | istockphoto.com | istockphoto.com | istockphoto.com |
| 000009321349 | | 000002783526 | 000015601215 | 000013623090 | 000014210559 | 000000825429 | 000007753196 |

| istockphoto.com | istockphoto.com | istockphoto.com | istockphoto.com | istockphoto.com | istockphoto.com | istockphoto.com | istockphoto.com |
| 000013532266 | 000016749480 | 000004239530 | 000002689230 | | 000002098320 | 000014570872 | 000016462400 |

Chapter 4

| istockphoto.com | istockphoto.com | istockphoto.com | istockphoto.com | istockphoto.com | istockphoto.com | istockphoto.com | istockphoto.com |
| | 000011338955 | 000006501522 | 000003080483 | 000017265205 | 000005299702 | 000000407292 | 000003386899 |

Chapter 5   **Chapter 6**

| istockphoto.com | istockphoto.com | istockphoto.com | istockphoto.com | istockphoto.com | istockphoto.com | istockphoto.com | istockphoto.com |
| 000012061829 | 000016850262 | 000018079393 | 000001478718 | 000012655395 | 000003919934 | 000002783526 | 000012979435 |

The iStockphoto images that appear on these pages were used to enhance the presentation of the book. You can find the exact photo at iStockphoto.com by conducting a search using the unique number code for the image.

Chapter 7

Chapter 8

istockphoto.com 000002295948

istockphoto.com 000001679350

istockphoto.com 000002743609

istockphoto.com

istockphoto.com 000003062749

istockphoto.com 000017473312

istockphoto.com 000016850256

Chapter 9

istockphoto.com 000000761342

istockphoto.com 000002187504

istockphoto.com 000002677242

istockphoto.com 000004994105

istockphoto.com 000002310227

istockphoto.com 000006160804

istockphoto.com 000003685771

Chapter 10

istockphoto.com 000001589846

istockphoto.com 000013344347

istockphoto.com 000018073953

istockphoto.com 000016850259

istockphoto.com 000016850258

istockphoto.com 000018073949

istockphoto.com 000018074557

Chapter 11

istockphoto.com 000000071701

istockphoto.com 000005896614

istockphoto.com 000007777554

istockphoto.com 000004927853

istockphoto.com 000004344227

istockphoto.com 000016864449

istockphoto.com 000009032551

Cover photo

by Alex Bramwell
istockphoto.com
000003043850

Index

Garr Reynolds travels the world giving keynote addresses and short-form presentations on several topics related to simplicity in design, communication, and daily life.

Garr's Presentation Zen™ seminars are popular worldwide and a good place to learn how to incorporate the principles of restraint, simplicity, and naturalness into your work.

THANK YOU

For more information please visit:
www.presentationzen.com

For inquiries regarding speaking engagements or training, please e-mail *book@garrreynolds.com*.

presentationzen

storyboarding ✦ sketchbook

Ideally suited to use alongside one of Garr Reynolds's books or his video, the high-quality **Presentation Zen Sketchbook** (ISBN: 0-321-73479-3, $14.99) includes blank pages for jotting down notes, creating mind maps, or brainstorming. It also includes pages with blank boxes that are sized for small sticky notes to storyboard your presentations.

Inspirational quotes from Garr's book **Presentation Zen** are sprinkled throughout the journal to help inspire you while you prepare and clarify your next presentation's content, purpose, and goals.

Learn more at www.peachpit.com/garrreynolds